STRANGE TALES

OF THE IMPOSSIBLE

PUBLISHING

For Uncle Joe, who never made me feel like a black sheep.

TABLE OF CONTENTS

A BRIEF
WORD ON
CONSCIOUSNESS

When most people think of consciousness, they think of one of three commonly accepted dictionary definitions: either the state of being awake and aware of one's surroundings, the awareness or perception of something by a person, or the fact of awareness by the mind of itself and the world. These definitions seem simple enough, describing the basis for understanding and interacting with our environment. And they are simple, right up until we really try to understand them.

Nobody can seem to agree on what exactly consciousness is or where it comes from. Some, like scientific materialists, think it arises out of the complexities of our brains; a reaction to stimuli that forms an illusion of something more. Still others, such as adherents of biocentrism, posit that consciousness creates the universe, and that without it nothing we observe would exist, at least not in the state in which we observe it. Even more speculation exists within a variety of other disciplines, too, regarding the nature of consciousness and whether it sits exclusively in the human brain, including the conundrum of, if it does exist outside of our bodies, does it do so as a projection from the brain or does it originate from outside of us?

Oxford psychologist Stuart Sutherland defined consciousness as "The having of perceptions, thoughts, and feelings; awareness. The term is impossible to define except in terms that are unintelligible without a grasp of what consciousness means. Many fall into the trap of equating consciousness with self-consciousness—to be conscious it is only necessary to be aware of the external world. Consciousness is a fascinating but elusive phenomenon: it is impossible to specify what it is, what it does, or why it has evolved. Nothing worth reading has been written on it," and after seeing the many divisions within science and philosophy that have arisen out of the subject, I can see why. With so little known about the nature of consciousness, I hope you won't mistake the speculations in this work for ardent beliefs on my part. Although I do hope, by the end, you might agree that they were worth reading.

INTRODUCTION

Early 20th century collector of weird stories Charles Fort had something he called "damned data," which he used to describe basically any information that leading scientific and religious authorities found inconvenient to their paradigms. It could mean anything from reports of lights in the sky to rains of frogs, so long as the phenomenon was being actively ignored by people with a vested interest in it not existing. Much of what we investigate in The Singular Fortean Society is similarly damned; inconvenient and ignored by the modern era's prevailing modes of thinking.

That's why our mission statement says we're ***"increasing what's imaginable by investigating the impossible."*** We don't believe in letting someone else elbow us aside just because what we're saying isn't popular. This isn't about achieving celebrity or conforming to any misguided philosophy of ignorance. We believe we owe it to the witnesses with whom we've spoken—and to ourselves—to share the stories we've collected in a way that is authentic to the experiences of those who lived them. By investigating and relating these supposedly impossible experiences, perhaps we can expand that which is found acceptable in our culture's collective imagination.

We don't claim to know the truth behind paranormal phenomena, but we're happy to speculate in the tradition of Fort, who after all did say that "one measures a circle, beginning anywhere." There is some weird connection between these phenomena, even if we can't exactly put our finger on it right now. And because of that connection, whatever it is, by studying any aspect of the unexplained we can understand something about the rest of it.

To that end, collected within this work are a variety of strange tales. Some of these tales are of our own experiences, while others come from the ardent testimony of witnesses with whom we've spoken. These stories describe a wide spectrum of fortean phenomena; everything from UFOs to aliens to ghosts to cryptids to high strangeness that ferociously defies categorization. We've recorded them and put them on the record as openly, honestly, and accurately as we are able, so please join us in investigating the impossible. We're happy to have you.

CHAPTER I

NEAT, PLAUSIBLE, AND WRONG

Explanations exist; they have existed for all time; there is al-
ways a well-known solution to every human problem—neat, plausible,
and wrong. - H.L. Mencken

One of the things I remember most about being a kid is being afraid. Every night I knew that no matter what I did, there was a
chance that the things haunting me would come out, and if they did,
there wasn't a thing I could do about it. I tried to stay up late, knowing
that they usually came while I was asleep, but I had to sleep eventually.
I tried hiding—both by concealing myself under my blankets and by
finding out-of-the-way places to sleep—but the former never worked
and the latter was just another temporary solution.

Inevitably, at some point, I would be in my bed, only to be awoken by the feeling of hands on me—pushing, prodding, poking me pain-
fully in my sides. Even worse were the images of large, ovaloid heads
with black eyes like the vacuum of space floating above me, and the
terror I felt lying in bed before it would happen, looking at my bedroom
window, somehow knowing that's how they got in, not wanting to stare
but unable to stop obsessing. And then there were the shadows.

I saw what can best be described as shadow people throughout
my childhood and ongoing into adulthood, along with the occasional
apparition. I might see shadowy forms flit from room to room in the
house, or duck behind the shed while I mowed the lawn. I think it's
possible that I mostly witness them simply going about their business,
with the most powerful interactions coming when I interrupt them or get
in their way. Such an interruption came one night in my early twenties.
Naturally, I was in bed.

I am awake. I was asleep a moment ago, but I'm definitely awake
now, although I'm not certain I'm supposed to be. I know I can

move, since I am able to rotate my head to the left, but I don't think it's a good idea to move too much, because I'm floating a couple of feet above my bed.

My bedroom is dark, but not completely so. The ambient light of the suburbs allows me to see the outline of its contents. My weight bench is there, and so is my dresser, and in front of them, part of the darkness is darker than the rest. This part is roughly human-shaped, and right next to me.

I am not afraid. I suppose I ought to be, but I'm not. I'm not certain that the human-shaped darkness knows that, since it reaches out its hand and places it comfortingly on my chest. I can still feel it today, every time I think about what happened.

It places its hand on my chest, and I'm slowly lowered back down to my bed. I don't remember the initial levitation—I assume that it most likely happened while I slept—I only recall being lowered back down. It is as though I'm being returned from somewhere, laid gently back in my bed, and my sudden wakefulness has interrupted the process in its final stage.

After I am once again lying on my bed, it finally occurs to me that I'm on top of my comforter. I never sleep on top of my comforter. I certainly hadn't fallen asleep that way. The shadow, having returned me to my repose, is gone; vanishing suddenly as I reach the bed. I lie there supinely while reflecting briefly on the oddity of the encounter before returning to sleep. It may seem strange that I was able to fall back asleep at all, let alone so quickly, but at this point in my life, I was so used to these kinds of events that I had learned to shrug them off. I wasn't hurt, and there didn't seem to be any important message. In fact, were I to hazard a guess, I don't think the intention was for me to be awake for any of it.

Close to 20 years later, the memory is still fresh in my mind. I can't explain it. My head fills with the static of cognitive dissonance whenever I try. I was witness to the laughably, shamefully impossible. To my mind, a shadowy figure presided over me levitating above my bed. That's what I remember.

Nighttime visitations are not unique to my experience. They've been with us for as long as we've had words to tell stories of them. We're a species under nocturnal siege by old hags, faeries, succubi, ghosts, extraterrestrials, and a thousand other, even stranger, creatures that all seem to have one thing in common: they love accosting us when we're at our most vulnerable.

Some would explain away these experiences as a trick of the mind. Our brains, once trusted allies, turned against us to exploit our deepest fears. Sleep paralysis, and hypnagogic and hypnopompic hallucinations—as popularized by the current paradigm of scientific materialism—are common explanations for instances of late-night harassment.

Sleep paralysis is what happens when we are awake but shouldn't be. The associated hallucinations occur either while falling asleep (hypnagogic), or upon waking up (hypnopompic). During an episode of hypnopompic sleep paralysis, one awakens without the ability to move, but with conscious perception of one's surroundings. Often the person experiencing the event is in a state of terror and aware of a presence in the room. I'm unsure if the terror is a function of the sleep paralysis, or a perfectly reasonable response to the situation.

The paralysis, at least, is explainable. While asleep, it is necessary for our bodies to prevent themselves from acting out all manner of dangerous activities in which we might be participating during REM sleep. It is for this reason that our brains secrete a neurotransmitter called glycine, which paralyses our muscles while we sleep. Thus, if one were to wake up before the REM cycle is complete one would find one's muscles still firmly in the grip of this normally helpful chemical.

The hallucinations attributable to sleep paralysis are a bit more complicated. They are eerily similar from person to person, and yet are often interpreted in vastly different ways. One man's old hag is another man's succubus. For now, I think it's best that I concentrate on what they most often have in common.

There is a feeling of a presence in the room, even before the person experiencing it can see what it is that's about to terrify them. Once the creature comes into sight, the unfortunate victim, still paralyzed, is then subjected to any one of a variety of unsettling tactile sensations. The one reported most regularly is that of being sat upon, but other people have described being grabbed or even held down. The victim might try and scream, but no sound comes out. The spell is broken once they can make even the tiniest movement, and things appear to return to normal.

Understandably afraid, it is perfectly normal for someone to stay awake for hours afterward, afraid that the event might be repeated. All in all, a genuinely unsettling experience. Unfortunately, sleep paralysis and hypnopompic hallucinations aren't the umbrella explanations that materialism wishes they were. They certainly don't explain what happened to me, and in that, I am not alone.

A friend of mine once came to me with an interesting experience—this is a common occurrence when people discover you investigate such things, everybody has a story they're just waiting to feel comfortable enough to share. So, my friend is awakened one night by a sharp pain in her knee, the one closest to the edge of the bed. She's had several knee surgeries, but this was unusual. This wasn't the achiness of a sore knee.

As she is roused from slumber a strange vision comes into focus: the figure of a four-foot-tall, white, glowing orb. Although she was immediately frightened, she somehow sensed that the orb had good intentions. Through some inexplicable communication, she understood that this being was fixing the cartilage in her knee. A short time after this realization, the enigmatic entity morphed into what she described as a "cat-like" creature and she fell back asleep very quickly, in a manner she described as "like when you're being put under for surgery." The being was still present as she sank into unconsciousness. The next morning, she remembered the events vividly, and says she felt a "bit nauseous and dizzy." Her knee, however, felt great.

My friend didn't experience sleep paralysis, and neither did I. We weren't hallucinating, and neither of us is making this up. First and foremost, we weren't paralyzed. There was movement involved for us both, but we also decided not to move any more than was necessary to observe our situation.

Nor do either of our experiences have any of the trademarks of sleep paralysis-induced hypnopompic hallucinations. They were too prolonged, and lacked the sudden disappearance triggered by movement that is present in an incidence of hypnopompic sleep paralysis. Not to mention that in both cases, we eventually went calmly back to sleep-- although not necessarily of her own free will in my friend's case.

And, of course, there is the distinct lack of terror. That, combined with the paucity of paralysis in both experiences, rules out sleep paralysis and its associated hallucinations as the cause of the events. Once sleep paralysis is discarded as an explanation, one must admit that both events lack any other trigger for a supposed hallucination. As to the veracity of our claims, well, I believe us. I know I'm not lying, and when interviewing my friend, I was completely convinced of her sincerity.

Without the popular medical explanation, I am left to wonder what happened. I can't help but focus on the casual nature of the events; in both instances it seemed like we weren't meant to be awake. It is as though a process, which exists independently outside of us, was accidentally interrupted. I can't help but imagine what it would have been like had I watched from outside my body. Perhaps I would have seen myself levitated off the bed and taken away, or merely witnessed my prone body used as an unwitting magician's assistant to be floated in the air for a hidden audience.

Regardless of whatever weird use might have been found for my unconscious form, the experiential evidence points to an external cause for the phenomenon. What that might be remains a mystery. Like so many of my experiences, it checks boxes from multiple paranormal categories. As tempting as it might be to capitulate to the comfort of categorization—because after all, fear is born of uncertainty—I simply cannot. This experience, on the surface, could be attributed as easily to a meddling spirit as it is an interloping alien. Despite other, more traditionally "alien," experiences I've had, it remains difficult for me to simply handwave everything together into the category of alien abduction. Especially when examined in the context of another, equally baffling experience had at around the same age as my nighttime levitation.

The ghosts of furniture burn for a few seconds when I flip off the light switch. The dining room is perfectly dark; the kind of absolute darkness that can only exist as an immediate contrast to a recently extinguished light. It's a dazzling, brilliant darkness that envelopes you completely and leaves you senseless.

My parents have made it clear that the light from the dining room disturbs their sleep slightly less than closing their bedroom door at night, but still enough to be unacceptable, so this is a black maze I've grown accustomed to navigating. Countless repetition has taught me where to step to avoid the table and chairs, which floorboards creak, and how to find the entrance to the living room without running into the wall. I've sidestepped the large wooden table, and I'm concentrating on slowly guiding my feet to just the right part of the rug to remain silent, when I feel something next to me.

I feel it in my gut, the same way you might feel that there's

The dining room at my parents' house is not where you'd expect to meet any monsters.

IMAGE: Emily Wayland

something in the dark before you trip on it. I know where everything is supposed to be in here, and absolutely nothing should be directly to my left at face-height…or breathing. The thing, whatever it is, radiates a casual malevolence, and the near side of my body tingles as I feel it draw close.

Although I cannot see it, the monster must be only inches from me when it hisses. It makes a sound like an angry cat, and I feel stale breath on my face. I haven't moved since I first felt its presence, but I steel myself, resolvedly whisper "leave me alone," and quickly cover the remaining distance to the living room, up the stairs, and into my bedroom. Not once do I think to turn on the lights.

Admittedly, with the absence of my sight I can only assume that this creature shared the shadowy visage common to the entities I had previously witnessed. But I feel comfortable in this assumption, without any evidence to the contrary, since many of my early interactions with the unknown were comprised of intrusions by these dark entities.

Whatever these things are, they seem to prefer the night for their unwelcome visits—possibly because they want to catch us asleep, or at least unawares. Such was the case for a young woman from Janesville, Wisconsin, with whom I spoke who told me that she'd encountered "a grey thing with black eyes" in her home during the spring of 2018.

The then 21-year-old woman had fallen asleep on the couch in her living room when she was awoken in the middle of the night by a bright light.

"I was woken up suddenly in the middle of the night from a very bright light shining through a small narrow window on the [front] door," she said.

The couch on which she had fallen asleep faces the front door, but the door itself is blocked from view by a wall. Anyone entering the home through the front door would need to turn immediately to their right and go around the wall to enter the living room.

"I had a roommate at the time, so I thought maybe it was her," the woman said. "As I stood up and slowly walked to the door, another thought came to my mind. What if it was a burglar?"

"I walked up to the door and suddenly, I was face to face with a grey thing with big black eyes standing there," she continued. "It honestly looked like your typical idea of what an alien would look like. It was slightly shorter than me, and I'm between 5'5" and 5'6"."

She screamed at the otherworldly intruder, and it shrieked back at her, its scream strange and birdlike.

"I screamed and it screamed back at me as if it didn't expect me to be there," she said. "I ran towards the kitchen and turned around towards my sister's bedroom."

It was then that she was struck by some sort of magnetic energy.

"It is very hard to describe," she explained. "Almost like electricity? Vibration? I was paralyzed. The entire room was lit up with that bright light and I was being pulled back to the couch."

She went on to describe the feeling caused by the energy as a "magnetic, tingling sensation," and said the light was bluish white in color.

Stuck in the magnetic energy's hold, the witness was pulled backwards towards the couch, her eyes closed in terror.

"I was floating," she said. "I was levitated above the couch I was originally sleeping in, and as soon as my body hit the couch, I 'woke up.' The living room was still as if nothing happened."

But the witness doesn't believe this was any dream.

"The entire time I was floating I told myself 'They're going to make you think this is a dream. They're going to make you think this didn't happen. It did happen. Don't forget," she emphasized.

She remembers her body bouncing off the couch as she was dropped unceremoniously onto it, and how she could feel its lumps press into her back as she landed. After she was returned to the couch, she opened her eyes to find that the living room "was still as if nothing happened."

The witness does not recall any gaps in memory or missing time during the event, nor did she find any out of place marks on her body afterward; although, admittedly, she did not specifically check for them.

Despite her surety she is still reluctant to discuss her experience.

"Everyone can just shrug it off as if it was just a dream," she said. "But I strongly feel that It was real. The fact that my initial reaction of someone coming inside was rational. The fact that I kept repeating to myself that this is real, it is happening, before I was brought back to the couch. It all seems and feels so real to me."

The witness explained that opening her eyes didn't feel like waking up in the traditional sense of a groggy return to awareness, but rather, saying that she "woke up" was the best way to describe the return from paralysis, and she was otherwise continuously aware of her situation and surroundings.

"I think what I said is what happened," she added. "I truly believe it happened."

I don't believe that young woman was any more asleep than I was during my own experiences.

Two other nighttime visitations that I've experienced remain fresh in my mind, both relatively recent and both fairly short, although no less impactful for their brevity.

The first was in early October of 2019. I was asleep and in the middle of a half-remembered dream about alien beings when I woke suddenly. I was on my side, unable to move, and someone—or something—was shining a bright, white light in my eyes. It reminded me most of the light from the ophthalmoscope my optometrist uses to examine the back of my eyes. As my conscious mind became aware of what was happening, I could feel that I wasn't meant to be awake, and just as quickly lost consciousness again.

Then, in February of 2020, I was awoken by my wife, Emily, tossing and turning. She mumbled that she was fine when I asked—she's a notorious sleep talker—so I laid back down on my stomach to go back to sleep. As I did, a black, scaly hand reached down in front of my face. I could feel other hands suddenly dig into my sides, trying to lift me. I pushed them away as best I could, frantically slapping at them, and they disappeared. I could feel myself making contact with the hands as I fought them off for what seemed like 15 to 20 seconds. It took me some time to fall asleep again after that.

Finally, I had a strange visitation while watching my parents' house a few years ago. It wasn't nighttime, but the experience is similar enough to the rest that I feel it should be included. I was on the couch one afternoon, watching a *Star Trek: The Next Generation* marathon on television, when I felt a heaviness come suddenly over me. I laid down and closed my eyes, unable to keep them open. Out of the darkness behind my eyes I saw a form approach—it was an ovaloid head with large, black eyes and otherwise subdued features that seemed to speak to me without moving its tiny slit of a mouth.

It said to me, "We are you."

After that, its seemingly telepathic message delivered, it withdrew, retreating in reverse of its entry. When it did, I opened my eyes, suddenly as spry as I had been prior to its intrusion. Even after much reflection, I'm still uncertain as to whether that line was meant as an explanation, confession, or accusation. The only thing apparent about it to me, much like the other experiences I've described, was that it represented some outside intrusion into my consciousness, and that hand-waving it away as a product of sleep-induced hallucination was inaccurate to my experience—a neat, plausible, and wrong solution to a very human problem.

CHAPTER 2

QUINN AND THE DAPPER APPARITION

To attempt any definitive explanation can often be a disservice to those who have witnessed the impossible, but certainly one as trite as sleep paralysis is especially reprehensible when dismissing the continued, impactful experiences of anyone whose childhood was defined by them. Such was the case with our friend Quinn, whose own encounters with the unknown were so like my own, only viewed through a separate facet of the fortean prism—a traditional haunting.

Emily and I sat down with Quinn in the summer of 2018 to discuss her experiences.

Storm clouds loomed threateningly overhead as Emily and I entered Madison Tap; I could tell by the way the wind had picked up that we were in for some weather, and soon. It's the perfect atmosphere for a ghost story, which was a beautiful synchronicity, since a ghost story was exactly why we were there. Our friend Quinn grew up surrounded by paranormal manifestations, and she had graciously offered to tell us her story.

"I had a pretty great experience," she said immediately as we sipped our drinks. "It wasn't like those scary ghost stories."

Quinn grew up in a "fairly haunted house" in a small town about 30 miles northwest of Madison, Wisconsin. The town was one of a handful that sprang up in the early 20th century around the nearby Badger Army Ammunition Plant, providing the munitions factory with plenty of workers.

This house was built by a prominent local family, and generations of them lived and died in the home and its surrounding area. And while she doesn't know if anyone has ever died in the house, there's no denying its significance to so many people over the decades.

"I think that just the sheer connection is probably what it is," Quinn speculated on the source of the haunting.

The house was similarly significant to our interviewee. Quinn's

The spirits being served here weren't the only ones on our mind this night.

IMAGE CREDIT: Emily Wayland

first paranormal encounter happened there when she was only three years old. She was lying in bed one night when she received a strange visitor—an event that is her first memory in the house.

"The earliest one I can remember I was laying in my bed in my bedroom, which was the former master bedroom," she said. "I was maybe three."

"I woke up in the middle of the night to a little boy singing the ABCs, and he had a train. And I remember just being like 'this is kind of weird.' I wasn't upset, but I just sat there and watched," she explained.

Quinn remembered rolling over in bed to see the boy, and she was sure she wasn't suffering from sleep paralysis. Naturally, she told her parents the next day, but the encounter was dismissed as the symptom of a child's overactive imagination. To Quinn the memory remained vivid; not something she would ascribe to fantasy. Her parent's denial of the experience only served to cement the memory in her mind.

"I think I have such a strong attachment to this memory because I remember telling them the next day and them saying, 'That didn't happen, you were dreaming.' And I remember being like 'no, I think it did. I think it did happen,'" she stated emphatically.

The next encounter she related took place when she was 10 or 11 years old. Quinn shared a room with her sister, where they slept in bunk beds—Quinn slept on the top bunk. Their beds were positioned against the wall opposite the bedroom's door, and a dresser stood a few feet away, abutting the perpendicular wall. A second, mirrored dresser was on the same wall as the door, directly across from where Quinn's head lay while in bed.

"I woke up, and I looked into the mirror, and I saw, clear as day, a man in a tuxedo; a nice, 1920s-style tuxedo," she asserted.

The era of the tuxedo was something she remembered specifically, because years later she was in class when she saw a picture of a man wearing such a suit, and the sight of it jogged her memory.

"I closed my eyes, and I opened them again, but he was still there. He didn't do anything. He didn't even make eye contact with me. I couldn't very clearly see his head, it was pretty much just like a tuxedo," she continued.

Quinn tried closing and opening her eyes several times, and each time the mysterious tuxedo-wearing apparition remained.

"I was spooked," she admitted, and said that at that point she decided to simply cover her head with her blanket until she fell asleep.

This well-dressed mystery man was a recurring character in Quinn's haunting, one she saw on three separate occasions.

The next encounter with him happened when she was around 12 years old.

Quinn's bedroom was across a small landing from the stairs leading up from the first floor, a bathroom and another bedroom were to the right of her room on the perpendicular wall, and on the opposite wall from them were two more bedrooms—an entrance to the attic was next to the top of the stairs.

"Out of my bedroom I could see straight down the stairs, and I could see right into this other bedroom. There was one time when I was walking out of my bedroom and I was going down the stairs, and I saw, out of the corner of my eye, the guy wearing the tuxedo in that bedroom," said Quinn.

Her final encounter with the tuxedo man, however, was one that she could have done without.

She was 18 or 19 years old at the time.

"I was sleeping in the attic. I woke up in the middle of the night, and the neighbor's dogs were barking," Quinn said. "I rolled over, and he was standing above me. There was no face, there was just kind of a grey swirl."

The ethereal being's body was simply a misty, grey, humanoid form, although the tuxedo itself was clear and detailed.

Quinn had hoped that perhaps the phenomenon was strictly a part of her childhood but seeing the tuxedo-wearing ghost after adulthood convinced her of the startling reality of her experiences, and quite frankly, it frightened her.

"And I have never slept at my parent's place since then," she said.

Her time at that house seemed to have been filled with unusual occurrences, and Quinn carefully recounted much of the phenomena she experienced.

"I would see shadows of kids, or hear kids—I say kids, but really I'd hear little feet running around upstairs when I was the only one home," she said.

"I used to be a terrible sleeper as a kid...obviously. I would go downstairs and watch TV in my parent's living room, and when you're lying on the couch you can't see the bottom of the stairs even if the door is open," Quinn explained. "There would be times when I'd be watching

TV and I would hear...you know when kids jump down the stairs and there's kind of like a grunt? I would hear that. It would be around 2 or 3 a.m. in the morning and I would hear that."

Another physical manifestation that stood out to her involved the seeming manipulation of a child's bouncy ball.

"In my bedroom we had a circle rug in the middle of the room, and one time there was a bouncy ball on the mirrored dresser across from the bed," Quinn recounted. "The bouncy ball rolled off the dresser in the middle of the night. I was probably eight or nine. I woke up to it bouncing, and I was waiting for it to stop, but it never did—I noticed it was maintaining its height. I threw it out of the room through the open door, and I heard it hit the stairs. I closed the door, and I was spooked, so I turned the light on and read a book until I fell back asleep. I woke up later, and that bouncy ball was in the middle of the circle rug."

And to add to the number of unsettling experiences already attached to her childhood bedroom, Quinn would sometimes wake up to see grey, misty phantoms walking through the walls of her home.

"There were other times when I'd be asleep, and I'd wake up, and I would see people walk through walls," she said. "They were ambiguous people, so I couldn't tell you what their gender was, but they clearly weren't my mom or dad."

Quinn's siblings had similar experiences as children but have since recanted.

"She said, 'Well, you know ghosts aren't real,'" Quinn said her sister told her prior to the interview. "And I said, 'actually, no, I'm quite positive of the alternative.'"

Not all her family was so dismissive; Quinn told us her aunt has been supportive of her experiences.

"She's always been the one who believed me," she said of her aunt. "I was always able to go to her, and she would say 'yeah, your house is kind of spooky.'"

Similarly, Quinn told us that her friends would often tell her they had an uncomfortable feeling in the house.

Quinn has also had quite a few psychic experiences in her life, and likely, they're connected to what she experienced in that old house. It's something she said she'd like to reclaim as part of her identity.

These experiences were a very personal affair for Quinn, and she knows what she experienced—if not necessarily the root cause of the phenomenon. Whatever it was, it was weird, and that weirdness has imprinted itself on her in the way it does all of us who experience it. We sometimes fight it and long for normality, but ultimately the strangeness in our lives moves back in as inexorably as the tide. Quinn, for her part, told us she was done fighting who she is.

"When you're 18 or 19 the last thing you want to be is weird," she said. "I really pushed it down and pushed it away. I'm just getting to a point now where I can not only be cool with it, and talk about it, but maybe get back to that place."

We spent some more time chatting about several other strange subjects, but eventually the hour drew late, and we all had our own houses to haunt, so we walked out into the night and said our goodbyes. It's always invigorating for me to discuss the impossible with another experiencer, especially one as intelligent and put-together as Quinn. I remember distinctly in that moment feeling as though Emily and I were on the cusp of something important, a revelation, if you will. It was only later that it really struck me. The footsteps, the apparitions, the night-time visitations—in so many ways, these phenomena mirrored what I and others had experienced. For Quinn it was a tuxedo-wearing ghost and for me it was shadow people, for others it's been grey aliens and even stranger things.

CHAPTER 3

RUDE AWAKENINGS

So often, for some esoteric reason, these impossible events occur while we're asleep, or at least, that's how they begin. As though whatever otherworldly intelligence is behind the various phenomena knows when we're at our most vulnerable, and that a sleeping person suddenly awoken is an almost perfectly captive audience. Such was the case with a friend of mine who woke suddenly one night to find something very unexpected in the woods of northern Wisconsin.

He was camping with his family on private land roughly 65 miles south of Lake Superior, near Wisconsin's northern border, on July 28th, 2018, when he arose out of a "dead sleep" at around 3 a.m. to see a floating cloud of glowing golden lights. The lights appeared to be hovering near a lantern he'd left out prior to retiring for the evening.

To my friend's credit, he had the presence of mind to do what many witnesses do not and grabbed his cellphone, managing to shoot about a two-minute video of the phenomenon.

"[The lights] had a lot of smaller spots that floated around, zig zagged, and left glowing lines in the air inside this aura of gold color," he told me. "And then larger, brighter, golden lights that winked in and out, and sort of moved around but slower, which is about all you can see in the video."

The unusual aerial display lasted for around 15 minutes, at which time the lights disappeared.

"They winked out in the same place, the smaller ones first and then the big ones," he said. "Since they were appearing and disappearing it was more like they just went out one by one and didn't come back. Then the entire golden aura/blob went out that contained the lights."

The area in which the lights appeared was northeast of their campsite, and a hill obscures the only house in that area, which stands about half a mile from the site—meaning the lights could not have come as a result of distorted houselights. Otherwise, the campsite exists within nothing but hundreds of acres of woods and water.

Historical weather data from the date and location of the sighting showed that the temperature at the time was hovering near 47 degrees, which is much cooler than fireflies prefer, making it unlikely that the glowing insects were responsible for the sighting. Fireflies prefer warm, humid air, and are significantly less active when the temperature dips below 60 degrees; they also don't often swarm in such tight, cloud-like formations.

"[There were] no insects really," he reported. "Normal flies during the day, but no biters and almost no skeeters. Then at night, nothing."

Other natural phenomena like ball lighting and swamp gas can likely be ruled out, since they do not appear as dozens of tiny individual glowing lights, but rather as a single object.

My friend and his family do stay regularly at the site, and while he promised to investigate the phenomenon further should he see it again, so far, he hasn't had the opportunity.

"If I see it again, I'll hit it with a high-powered flashlight," he said. "But I had that sitting on my truck."

A journey he was not particularly enthusiastic about making under the circumstances.

"Believe it or not, getting out in the woods with 'something' isn't really an attractive thing when you're there," he explained.

I don't blame him.

Almost two years later, I heard from a woman who had awoken to a somewhat different sort of light. This one was inside of her home in Kenosha, Wisconsin.

I'd been put in touch with Jane in February of 2020 by Mike Lucas, an old friend from my days volunteering as a field investigator for the Mutual UFO Network (MUFON). She told me that she had awoken one late summer night in 2009 to find a "charcoal-colored cloud shape" emanating an "amber light" near the ceiling of her bedroom.

"It was probably late summer 2009. It was a long time ago, and it only happened that one time. Other things have happened in that house, but this is the one thing I can't categorize," Jane said to me over the phone. "It was in the middle of the night. I was woken up. I don't typically wake up at night. I can't say that it was a noise or anything that woke me up. I just woke up."

I'm a very pragmatic, practical, logical person, and what I saw in the room, I couldn't put any reason to it. At the foot of the bed, near the ceiling, there's a corner wall there with built-in dressers and next to the built-in dressers there's a window that had a window air conditioner in it. There were little cracks of light on both sides of where the window air conditioner fits into the window.

So, up in that corner, on the ceiling, there was an object that, I would say, was probably four feet wide by two or three feet tall, sitting near the top of the ceiling. It was a charcoal-colored cloud shape, but it wasn't cloud-like. Cloud-shaped meaning it had puffiness around it, but it looked solid, a solid charcoal color. Inside of it, there looked like there was an amber light, kind of trying to emanate from the inside out. You could see gradations of this amber light from the inside to the outside of the charcoal cloud.

If I had a shoe or something that I could have thrown at it, I swear it would have bounced off, because that's how solid it looked. But the amber light from the inside, that's what got me.

Immediately I thought, "I'm dreaming. I must have woken up during a dream and that's still part of my dream. Okay, I'll just close my eyes and when I wake up it will be gone."

I closed my eyes, and I couldn't go back to sleep. I peeked up and it was still there. I'm rubbing my eyes, pinching myself. I'm awake.

I'm one hundred percent awake and I'm looking at this thing going, "I don't know what that is."

So, I turned over, and maybe 20 minutes later I thought it's going to fade away because clearly if it's not part of a dream it must be a hallucination. 20 minutes go by, I turn over, it's still there. It's not moving. There's nothing about it that's mobile or foggy or anything. It's just hanging there solid.

Eventually, I must have fallen asleep, because the next morning it wasn't there. I wasn't afraid.

I wasn't calling anybody saying, "Something strange happened last night."

It wasn't like that.

Jane was at a loss to explain the event, although it wasn't the only seemingly paranormal phenomenon she'd experienced in the house.

"I've had other occurrences in the house," she said. "I'm the third owner of the house, after it was built in 1948. I learned from the grand-daughter of the first owner that her grandfather, who had built the house, had passed away in the kitchen. That much I do know."

"If you want to talk spiritual stuff, I've always felt protected in the house," she continued. "I bought the house myself, and a few years later I was married for just a short time. During that time, there was a lot of chaos and drama and psychological problems in the house. A lot of stress and a lot of illness."

Also, during that time, in the summer of 2002, a peculiar event involving an electric typewriter occurred—one for which she still doesn't have an explanation.

My then husband had an office in the basement, and one day when I was home alone, I heard this noise. I went down into the basement, and here it was his electric typewriter going nuts. It was just typing over and over. It was weird.

I thought, "Well, something's wrong with it. Why is it on and typing away? There's no paper in it."

Then I looked at the on/off switch and it was in the off position. It was plugged in, but it was off.

When my husband came home, I said, "You're never going to believe what happened. That typewriter of yours just started typing by itself."

He asked, "Wow, was there paper in it?"

I said, "No, there's no paper in it."

He said, "Put some paper in it."

I said, "It's not going to happen again. It was an electronic glitch. It's not going to happen again."

He insisted, "Put some paper in it."

I put some paper in it.

Within the week—he was home the second time—I heard it go-ing off again. We both ran downstairs, and it was typing away. I wish I was making this up, because I'm shaking now thinking about it, but at the time I wasn't afraid. I just thought it was a glitch.

It was typing letters in a sequence, and when it stopped, because he unplugged it, again, it was in the off position. I pulled the paper out, and he's trying to make a pattern out of the letters to figure out if it says anything. It didn't have any vowels. He was trying to see if it would make any sense if you put vowels in it. He thought it was saying 'leviathan' over and over again.

I said, "I don't know, it could be."

Jane told me that the sequence of letters was LVTNC.

The repeating sequence was in an italic font, something Jane's husband at the time said was impossible.

"I could say that there was something wrong with the typewriter, I could easily accept that, but then again, it happened two times and I've always felt this protective spirit in the house," she said. "[My ex-husband] told me that the script it was written in wasn't in that typewriter. It was a plain, one-script typewriter from the 1970s. It only had one font, and this was a scripted font. I said, 'It can't be. You have to have two fonts in here. One italic and one normal.' But he claimed there was no italic font in the typewriter. I thought maybe he just didn't know that he had it."

Others have experienced strange phenomena in the house, too, she said, including her niece's now ex-husband whom Jane had hired to work on the drywall in her basement.

"He didn't like to work in the house by himself, because he said he felt like my house had spirits or something and he would hear them when he was in the basement," said Jane.

As for herself, Jane had only one other strange experience in the house.

"The only other time I can remember was—it's a cape cod style home, so the upstairs is like a double room, like a bunked-out dormer style—I was upstairs one night, and I heard some clunking and clanking sounds coming from the bathroom," she said. "I very carefully went downstairs and investigated. It sounded like something metal hitting the inside of the bathtub. When I checked it out, there was nothing out of place."

Jane added that she later found out the house's second owners had a son who passed away in the house.

But these experiences had been with Jane prior to buying the house in Kenosha.

One night at 9 p.m., in the summer of 1992, she encountered an invisible phenomenon in her one-bedroom apartment in Montgomery, Illinois, that would spark continued harassment by unknown forces for the rest of her stay there.

I had spent the evening with some friends from church—it was a summer night—I came home, and I had a laundry basket in the bathroom, and I went to toss my socks in the laundry basket. You know how much force and effort it takes to throw something two feet to land in the basket. So, I went to toss the socks, and they were going through the air, and they hit like this invisible wall. Vertically, the socks dropped short of the basket and my eyes just bugged out of my head. How did that happen? It was like midair they hit a vertical, invisible wall and slid down short of the basket. That was weird.

From that moment on, that night, there was something there. It haunted me until I had to move out. It was an ongoing darkness. It didn't let me sleep. I just felt kind of harassed. There were other phenomena. The phone would ring many times of the day and night, and there would be no one there. Was that somebody harassing me or was it something else? I don't know, but there was never anybody else on the other line.

These strange phenomena, it turned out, had been with Jane and her family since she was a child.

One of Jane's younger brothers, Jim, experienced a series of events as a child in their Kenosha home that left him afraid of the basement, despite it being fully furnished, including a rec room.

"There are four of us kids," she said. "The boys' bedroom has the most activity, even now. My brother Jim, he's maybe the sensate or intuitive in the home, he took on everybody's emotional energy. He was the troublemaker and the black sheep. I think he couldn't handle all of the sensations that he was experiencing all of the time."

His bedroom was—or the boys' bedroom was—the hub of all the activity, too. He would wake up in the basement in a panic. He was always afraid of the basement, I think a lot of kids are, but he would be running out of the basement, saying he woke in the basement after a man had carried him down there.

My mom and dad were like, "No, you were sleep walking."

I don't know if they ever had any proof of him sleepwalking, but that would be the only explanation for waking up in a room that you don't want to be in.

I asked him about this as an adult, not too many years ago, because something else happened to me in the house as an adult. I had to ask him, "What happened? Because everybody was saying you were sleepwalking."

He said to me, "Jane, I'm telling you now, I'm a grown adult and I'm telling you that I was not sleepwalking. A man carried me to the basement."

He had had things happen to him where he'd reach under the bottom bunk of their bunk beds to get something, and I don't remember if he said he felt a man's bare arm or a man's arm grabbed him, but it was one or the other. But he felt a body under the bed.

I know that he said that [the man] was hairless, he didn't have body hair, like his arms were bare. I don't know if he had too much of a visual.

Even now, he doesn't want to be in the basement by himself.

Jane isn't particularly bothered by the basement, it's the guest room—her brothers' former room—that she doesn't like.

One series of events in the room, experienced while staying there to assist her aging parents, she found particularly disturbing.

"I don't mind the basement, but what I don't like is the guest bedroom that used to be the boys' bedroom," she said.

Without any preconceived notions about anything in the room, because at the time I still believed my brother had been sleepwalking and imagining things, one night while lying in bed I felt someone patting me on the head. Like a loving gesture, you know, pat, pat, pat on my head.

And I'm thinking, "That's not a fly, that's not a hair out of place, that is a hand patting me on the head."

I flipped around, and there's no one there, but my heart is pounding and I'm thinking, "Who is here?"

You don't sleep after that very well. It happened more than once, maybe three or four times.

Finally, I said, "You've got to go. You can't be here."

One time I was actually sitting on the hide-a-bed—I've seen this in movies, I've seen this in TV shows, it doesn't happen in real life, but it did—it was like someone sat down next to me. The mattress went down, like someone was sitting next to me. When that happened, I thought we'd better get somebody in here to tell the spirit to go.

Two live-in caregivers, hired to assist her parents, also experienced the strange head patting, according to Jane.

One of the caregivers was let go after resuming a drug habit, and the other later died in the bedroom of a heart disorder.

Jane also said that at a young age she would experience extra sensory perception (ESP), at times being aware of things that hadn't yet happened or had happened outside of the range of her normal senses.

These phenomena, as experienced by Jane and others, don't occur exclusively when we're in bed, although they may begin there, and when they do bleed into the normal waking hours, it's often with terrifying results.

I first spoke to North Carolina resident Bet Dotson in early 2019 about a series of unsettling events that had begun decades earlier.

The first such incident occurred one night in 1981 when Bet was just 13 years old, and she woke up around 2 a.m. to a bright light flooding her room.

"I thought the mountain [near my house] was on fire," she told me.

She looked out her window and saw a cigar-shaped craft emitting twin beams of light, the sight of which left her paralyzed. Afterwards she said she suffered from symptoms of shock and fatigue, and that her body temperature was much higher than normal for some time following the event.

Not long after that, Bet said she had seen a shadowy figure with a "bird face" and "weird grin" while sitting at home in bed reading a book. She saw a shadow cross her hallway before the "thing" peered around the doorway into her room. She sat frozen in fear and the creature left without further incident.

But it was in 1986 that Bet had perhaps her most chilling encounter, when she was attacked by a bird-like creature while on her way to visit her sister in Silverstone, North Carolina.

"I was driving a VW Beetle to visit with my sister in Silverstone, which is off Highway 421," she said. "I was around 18 years old at the time."

"I stopped at a stop sign off 421 where my headlights were shining directly on a barn straight ahead," Bet continued. "I saw this winged, human-like creature running alongside the front of the barn. It was around six to seven feet tall, dark, [with] two arms, two legs, and

A sketch of the creature.

IMAGE CREDIT: Bet Dotson

huge wings."

She described the creature as "part bird, part man," and said it appeared to be wearing "combat boots."

"It freaked me out!" she added.

Bet sped away, only to discover the creature had given chase.

"I made a left turn and sped up, questioning what the heck I was seeing," she said. "I heard wings flapping, looked into my driver side mirror and could see this thing almost on top of my car following me. It kept up with my speed, which I would estimate at about 45 to 50 mph on a very curvy two-lane road. It followed behind and beside my vehicle for several miles."

The winged being continuously attacked her vehicle as she fled, during which time the car's electrical system was drained—a phenomenon commonly reported by witnesses of UFOs.

"My VW engine was sputtering and seemingly the battery was being drained. The headlights dimming as I nervously rounded curves," Bet said. "This winged thing was flying over and pretty much clinging to the driver's side of my car. It was hitting my car. It was smacking into it."

"I didn't understand why he was on the driver's side hitting my car," she continued. "Like I felt he was trying to get inside my vehicle. He was trying to get to me."

Bet doesn't remember what happened immediately after the attack and said that she later came to—still behind the wheel and driving—after four hours of missing time.

"I had missing time after rounding several curves," she said. "I don't know why or what happened after those curves, but I was further puzzled and lost. I saw a sign that read Camp Joy and I had no clue how I got off of my normal route. How did I get over here?"

Although she had left for her sister's around 8 p.m., it was after midnight by the time she returned home.

"When I got home and realized what the time was, I was further puzzled. The trip that generally took no more than 20 minutes to see my sister had taken four hours," said Bet.

"I was absolutely scared sick," she added. "When I finally made it back home, I was in tears."

Bet went on to tell me that she has suffered from multiple abduction experiences but doesn't like to talk about all of them out of fear that the entities involved will seek retribution.

1986 Winged Humanoid Encounter

A sketch of the winged being chasing Bet's car.

IMAGE CREDIT: Bet Dotson

A photo of Bet's VW Beetle taken shortly after the incident.

IMAGE CREDIT: Bet Dotson

As for the birdlike creatures she saw, Bet thinks those encounters could be related to UFO lore involving reptilians and hybrid experiments.

"Many people have asked me what I think I encountered; demon, mothman, and so forth. I think I encountered a half-bird, half-man experiment," she explained. "Winged creatures are somewhat fallen angel/Draconian. Some of them are experiments."

We'll find narratives like this pop-up time and again. I don't know if they're true or not—although I don't doubt that people believe in them—but regardless of their veracity, I think they serve an important function: understanding. It's important that we feel like we can study and categorize these phenomena, because the alternative is utterly paralyzing in its enormity. The idea that we might be interacting with something so vast, so completely alien, that we can't even see all of it, let alone understand it, is one I don't think we as a species are prepared to face.

Imagine encountering a being who exists in only two dimensions. We, as three-dimensional beings, would be able to pass in or out of its world at will, and all it would ever be able to see of us is the tiny sliver within the two-dimensional plane which it can perceive. Now, imagine encountering a being who exists in five or more dimensions. What would the sliver of them we're capable of perceiving look like? What if that sliver looks like whatever they want, or we want, or maybe even what they think we want? Or possibly any of the three, as is convenient for them at the time.

If these things, whatever they are, interact directly with and manipulate our consciousness, as they sometimes appear to do, then there doesn't seem to be a reliable way to really observe them—again, if we're even capable of fully doing so in the first place—at least, not with our physical senses. Maybe that's why they like to come at night, when our minds are drifting into altered states of consciousness; subtle psychic senses replacing our physical ones as our bodies rest. Maybe our consciousness, unlike our physical being, exists in more dimensions than we know, and devoid of the distractions which are endemic to the material world, can perceive the creatures who naturally exist in the same spaces it occupies. A state which makes us not only more perceptive, but perceptible, and thus more vulnerable.

It was nighttime when Olga had her first experience with a shadow person in her home in Rogers, Minnesota, a city roughly 10 miles northwest of Minneapolis. I spoke to Olga over the phone in November of 2020, after she had reached out to us through the Singular Fortean Society's email address.

According to Olga, the strange experiences began eight years prior when she was 72 and her grandson, Toby, was four.

It's only happened about four times, and for several years it hadn't happened, until just recently it happened again. First off, I don't believe in this stuff, I always believe there's a reasonable explanation for everything. That's always been my take on it. Most people see ghosts and this and that, and I think, there's got to be a reasonable explanation.

I'm on the phone one evening at around 10 p.m. talking with someone, and I was sitting in my living room, which faces the entryway, or foyer, and off the foyer, there's seven stairs going up and then seven stairs going down. It's a multilevel house. I glanced up, and this black thing comes down the stairs. It's shaped like a human, and my feeling was that it was male. I don't know why I felt that way. It was about 5'7" or 5'8" and shaped like kind of a husky male. It actually reminded me of my late husband. I mean the shape, you know?

It just glided. It wasn't walking, I didn't see any feet or anything. Part of the wall would have hidden it anyway, but from the gait or way it was moving, it was gliding. It glided down the stairs and disappeared around the railing, and probably went down into the family room.

I saw no eyes. It wasn't facing me, really, I was profile from it. It was solid. It seemed to me to be solid, because there's a railing there and I didn't see the railing through it. I couldn't see anything through this thing. I didn't see a shadow on the wall on the other side of it, either.

I tried to stay calm and finish my conversation. I quickly hung up and I thought, "Oh, Toby's upstairs, and that's where it came from."

So, I went and checked on Toby, and he was sound asleep. He was just four years old. The hallway light was on. I left it on all night, and I've been leaving it on all night ever since. I went to bed, and the next morning [around 7 a.m.] when I wake up, Toby's jumping into bed with me. That's not unusual, he would do that all the time. I have custody of him, his mother doesn't live here with us.

So, I said, "Okay, grandma's getting up."

I had to go to the bathroom, so I walked across the room towards my bathroom. He's right on my heels, and he jumps in there with me and slams the door. It kind of startled me. I didn't want to put anything into his head, because right away I thought of what I'd seen the night before.

I asked, "Oh, how come you're up so early?" I tried to be cheerful, because he looked really scared.

He said, "It was the door monster. The door monster woke me up."

I asked, "The door monster?"

He replied, "Yeah, the door monster."

I asked, "What did the door monster look like?"

"He was black," he said. He called it a "he."

"And he had red eyes. He was staring at us." And that's about all I got out of him. Then he was just repeating himself. I looked out of the bathroom towards my bedroom door, and of course there was nothing there.

That made me start believing. Why would he see the same thing I saw?

Olga told her son, Shawn, who was 52 at the time, but she said, "he just kind of blew me off."

That is until he had his own experience.

"Several weeks later, my son came running up from downstairs in the family room," Olga said. "He came running upstairs and said, 'Oh my god, call somebody, we need to have a séance or something. We have a ghost or something in this house.' I asked, 'What are you talking about?' He said, 'I saw that black thing, and it moves really fast.' He was all excited or upset about it, I'm not sure which. It was something we talked about for a while, but then it didn't show up again."

While, as of the time of this writing, Olga and Shawn haven't seen any more mysterious shadow people, at least one other family member has.

"Only a couple of weeks before I contacted you, my great-grandson spent the night, and he's about the same age as Toby," Olga said. "He stayed in the spare room, along with Toby. There are twin beds in there. The boys were each in a bed with a nightstand between them.

[My great-grandson] had stayed over before, and he always wakes up at night. The next morning, he told me, 'I saw something last night, grandma.' I asked, 'What did you see?' I wasn't expecting that, really, because we hadn't seen the thing in a few years. He said, 'It was black, shaped like a person.' I asked him if he'd seen any facial features, and he said, 'No, it looked like it was looking towards Toby. I didn't see its face. It was standing in our doorway, watching Toby.'"

Olga said that her great-grandson had turned over in bed, and "he was kind of squinting. His eyes were kind of half-open and half-shut, and he said he saw this black thing. Then he opened his eyes wider and saw the shape, and then it just disappeared on him. He said it seemed to be looking at Toby and looking away from him, but it seemed to know he was looking at it because it just left."

"The thing, the shadow person, it doesn't appear that often," she added. "It's been years. So, it's like it's back."

Although her reaction to her own sighting left her puzzled, Olga admitted to being disturbed by the being or beings.

"I don't understand my own reaction when I saw it. I don't know how I even got to bed or got to sleep that night. Normally, I think I would have stayed up all night," she said. "What really bothers me is that it seemed to focus on my grandson. Right now, my instincts tell me it's watching Toby for some reason. I wonder what interest this thing has in him."

Members of the family reported other unusual phenomena concurrent to the shadow person sightings, including strange, glowing orbs and phantom presences.

"We've only had [the shadow person sightings] happen four times, although other things have happened," Olga said. "My daughter said she saw an orb flying across our backyard. Toby said he saw one down in the family room, a white ball that went into the couch. My son said he saw a white ball with blue in the middle. I don't know where that one flew to."

"My son is feeling someone sitting on his bed—the weight of someone sitting on his bed at night," she continued. "He's been having these feelings that someone is in his room all the time at night. It's just feelings, nothing he's seen, but he says he's actually felt the bed move down like someone is sitting on it. He also felt someone whack him on both of his feet, and he sat up immediately. He said it's a good thing he had his pillow there, or his head would have hit the headboard or something."

According to Olga, the bedroom set in her son's room once be-longed to a neighbor woman who passed away, leading her son to spec-ulate that the presence might be related to some attachment she has with the furniture.

"He thinks it could be this guy's wife, bugging him because he's got the bedroom set now," she said.

Whether or not those experiences are related to the sightings of shadow people is open to interpretation, although Olga sees no reason why her home would be haunted.

"The house that we live in, I had this house built. This was a va-cant lot—a farm field, before we lived here," she explained. "So, it can't be from previous residents that I can think of. It was just a farmer's field, until he sold his land into development."

Regardless, there does appear to be some significance to certain areas of the house. Olga noted that the shadowy being "hasn't been seen in any other room than the hallway or the stairway," and Toby refuses to sleep in his bedroom.

"He won't sleep in his room anymore," she said. "He wants to sleep in [the spare room]. That room where his cousin and him were sleeping during the last sighting of this thing. That's where he sleeps every night now. He won't go back to his own room. I don't know if it's something to do with that room, but even before this happened, when I would put him to bed at night—we're talking two or three years old—he insisted I shut the closet door. He's afraid of that closet in his room, and I really don't know why. If he saw something there when he was little, I'm not sure. He's never said why he wanted the closet door shut. I kind of feel like something must have happened when he was sleeping in that room, because that closet door always had to be shut at nighttime."

Olga said that one her daughters also felt uneasy about the closet in Toby's bedroom.

"She's always been leery of that closet," she said. "I never put it together, because I never paid too much attention to her being scared of that closet because it wasn't her room anyway."

It's unclear to Olga what, if anything, those feelings might have to do with the shadow people seen in her home, or what the nature of that phenomenon might be.

She does, however, suspect that the being or beings could be intelligent in some way.

"[The being] disappears really fast, like it doesn't want to be seen," Olga said. "If it has a mind, I don't know. It seems like the minute someone sees it, it takes off. I don't know if it even knew I saw it, because it was coming down the stairs. It went down the stairs and around the railing and down again. I didn't see any eyes or anything, I was sitting more on the side of it. I don't know—if it is a real thing—if it even saw me."

Ultimately, the events experienced by Olga and her family remain a mystery, much like many of the subjects contained within this work, although they have served to expand her perspective.

"I'm to the point now where I'm thinking there may be other dimensions that we don't see, except on an occasion like this," she said. "That's the only thing I could think of, maybe it's from another dimension or something. I don't know."

Maybe expanding our perspective is the whole point.

It would be difficult to argue that Deshunda Johnson didn't have her perspective changed drastically by her experiences with the unknown.

I spoke to the 45-year-old delivery driver in September of 2020 about a series of UFO encounters she'd had in and around Madison, Wisconsin, beginning in 2001; although, as it would turn out, that wasn't the first time she'd experienced the impossible in her life.

Her sighting in 2001 took place in July or August, she said, at about 9 p.m.

My friend and I were going to work, driving on Stoughton Road [in Madison].

She said to me, "Look, Deshunda, what is that?"

I asked her what she was talking about. We were getting off of the Beltline Highway [onto Stoughton Road], going to work, and to the right in a wooded area that looks like a marsh—going towards Stoughton and McFarland—there was a green light that just shot straight up.

She asked me, "Did you see that?"

And I said, "Yes, I saw it."

I put my foot on the accelerator and took off. When I see stuff like that, the only thing I know is to take off.

Who's going to be in that marshy area shooting off firecrackers? There was no noise, we had our windows down because it was nice out.

"That was the first time I saw something like that," she said of the green light. "After that [my sightings] started. When we got to work, [my friend] said, 'You all won't believe what we saw.' I told her not to tell anybody because they'll think we're crazy. She told me, 'Deshunda, you know that wasn't a shooting star. Shooting stars come down, they don't shoot up.' I said, 'Yes, I know, and that's why I'm not saying nothing.'"

"The following week," she added. "Her daughter and her boyfriend said they saw the same thing."

Deshunda told me she wished she'd documented the sighting better.

"When you see it the first time, people think they won't see anything like that again, or pray they don't see it again," she said.

Her next sighting came in the summer of 2007.

"I had something strange happen to me over on McCann Road [in Madison, Wisconsin]," Deshunda said. "My son, he's the one who spotted it. It was above me."

We got out of the car after coming home from the grocery story, and [there was an object floating above me that] looked like a cloud. Actually, it was a cloud. There were no other clouds in the sky.

I told [my son], "Get the groceries out of the car."

We stayed just off of McCann Road in a townhouse.

He said, "Mom, look."

And I said, "Look at what?"

And he said, "Above you."

When I looked above my head, and I'm short, this thing was over my head and I... I don't know what happened. All I know is I was like thrown.

I said, "Get in the house."

My son, he almost hit the wall looking at it while trying to run into the house.

I didn't know what it was. But it was a cloud, there were no other clouds, and no cloud moves like that. It had four white lights circling inside of it. It hovered over me, and I kid you not, when I moved, it moved. It was close enough that I could touch it, but I was too scared. It was that low.

I ran into my house. I wasn't going to stand there anymore. There's no way I'm going to stand under something that I don't understand and don't know nothing about. We got into the house and that thing stood there for a minute. Then it moved to the backyard.

There were people in their backyard in the next neighborhood, and it moved over to between my yard and theirs and there were people there who had their phones out [who looked like they were taking pictures] and staring at it. As I was standing there, something told me not to go out there. I wasn't going nowhere.

It stayed there for over 20 minutes. It would not leave. It was like it was waiting for something.

After that, I'm always looking up.

"I called the police and asked them about the lights," Deshunda explained. "[The woman I spoke to] said they'd gotten some calls. I told her not to laugh at me. This is something strange, I've never seen nothing like this. She asked me what it looked like. I said you need to get somebody out here."

She said that, ultimately, the police did not visit the scene and no official report was made.

I couldn't corroborate her testimony using police records or by speaking with her old neighbors, given the lack of official reports and the time that had passed.

After this sighting, said Deshunda, "strange stuff just started happening."

She told me that she was awoken one night by what sounded like somebody running in her bedroom.

I woke up and my door opened— [it was previously open just a crack]—and all I heard were footsteps in my room. My heart just started pounding. I got up and thought maybe it's the dogs or something. I went downstairs to check, but the dogs were in the crate. I went in my sons' room, and they were asleep. I looked under the bed, and I didn't see anything.

I asked my boyfriend at the time, "Did you come in my room?"

He said no. He said he was out down the street. I asked him if he was sure, and he said yes.

"I told my landlord I had to move," she continued. "I had been there eight years. He asked me why I wanted to move. I couldn't tell him."

Deshunda's sightings continued July 7th, 2020.

I had to go to the back roads and drop off on County T off Sprecher Road. Way before I got there, off Mesta Lane, there was a light so bright that at first, I thought it was the sun. I'm at the stoplight, and I put my visor down.

I said, "That sun is bright!"

I looked at my map and see I have to go off County T, way out in the boondocks.

I head out there, and all of a sudden, I look to my right—after something said in my head "look to your right"—when I looked, an object was above the power lines, stationary. I had my windows half down. There was a man in a car close behind me, and I thought he had to being this. But when I looked again, his car was way behind me.

It felt as if I was moving, but not fast enough. I was staring at it; I couldn't keep my eyes off it. It had a green light at the bottom, it was black, a round dome, and I'm just looking at this light. That lasted for about two minutes. When I got the lady's food to her, I looked at the time and it was probably 8:06 or 8:07, but she said she'd ordered her food an hour ago. I was thinking, looking at the clock, that it's only 8:06 p.m.

I got home and I was still shaken up. My eyes were red and irritated from the brightness of the light.

A week later, she had another sighting in the same area.

I went to the ATM to get money out, and they just built these buildings right after I saw this thing off County T. I saw this green ball of light hovering over this building. It wasn't a bug, it looked like a sphere.

I said, "No, we're not doing this tonight."

I got in my car and left. [The green ball of light] went off towards East Towne Mall. Most people might follow it, but me, I'm going home. That's not the first time that I've seen those things. I don't understand why I'm seeing it.

The strange thing is, while I was driving, I said to myself, "If I ever see anything like that again, I'm going to go ahead and take a picture of it."

But it didn't happen that way.

Deshunda's most recent sighting occurred at approximately 9:15 p.m. on August 30th, 2020. She was in Stoughton delivering food near the intersection of Roby Road and King's Lynn Road.

When I looked at my app it said I was two or three minutes from the house. I was going through the neighborhood, when all of a sudden—this is not the first time this has happened to me—something told me to look to my left.

I just looked over and I said, "What in the?"

I said, "That plane is flying really low in its flight."

So, I slowed down, I saw kids in a group going across the street. I looked, and all of a sudden, I got nervous. I was just staring at it.

That's when I was like, "Uh-uh uh-uh, it's stationary. It's not moving."

All I could see were the lights flickering. It was over houses, and it wasn't that far from me—maybe three or four hundred feet. I know what I saw. It looked like it was multicolored—white, red, but it wasn't a bright red, it almost looked orange.

As I was looking at it, it just stayed in one spot. It looked black. I wanted to get out and take a picture of it, but all of a sudden, I got really nervous.

I said "Should I? No, I better get this lady her food."

I'm sitting in my car, just looking at it, driving slowly just looking at it.

As soon as I said "Okay, maybe it will be there when I get back."

I'm saying to myself, "No, just stop and take a picture, because nobody is going to believe you've seen some stuff like this."

I kept saying to myself, "No, that's a plane, that's a plane. I'm not seeing what I'm seeing."

The thing tilted up, and when it tilted, it was a triangle. It had a light at the top, and one on the bottom at each side. My eyes got bigger than my glasses. All I know is, when I saw what it did and I turned back, that thing took off. I put my foot on the gas and dropped that lady's food off.

It's as if it wanted me to see it, to say, "No, I'm not a plane."

That was not an airplane. Nobody can convince me.

She further explained that she had her car door open slightly but was afraid to get out because she thought the craft might approach her if she did.

According to Deshunda, the sighting lasted "a minute or two."

Shortly after this sighting, Deshunda spoke to a friend in Stoughton who said she'd "seen a lot of strange stuff out here."

Deshunda wondered if perhaps the craft were trying to communicate with her, and if that might somehow be tied to a series of psychic experiences she's had in her life.

"I'm very clairvoyant. I've had out of body experiences. I see auras around people, I see colors, and if they have certain colors then I don't go near them. I would tell my mom and she would tell me to shush. I never understood that. I thought that maybe there was something wrong with me," she said. "She told me she had the same thing, but she blocked it. You can tell people all day long, but they'll never understand."

Olga also told me about a strange psychic bond she had with her mother.

"My mother was kind of strange," Olga said. "I had a nightmare one night that I was in a wedding party, and I lost my bouquet of flowers, and I was crying. I was calling for my mommy. My husband shook me and woke me up. He asked, 'Why are you calling for your mom?' I just said, 'Oh, nothing.' And I went back to sleep. The next morning, 7 o'clock in the morning, she called and asked, 'Why did you wake me up last night? I heard you calling me.' That really blew me away, but mom was kind of that way, you know?"

I don't discuss it often—nobody likes a self-proclaimed psychic—but I've certainly had my share of psychic experiences. Mostly little things like knowing when someone has arrived before they've made their presence known or mentioning that I have a strong feeling I should call my mother, only to minutes later have her call me. Occasionally, I'll dream of something that will come to pass, but my life isn't terribly exciting, so it's often of perfectly mundane tasks, like waiting in line at the drug store or a small series of events playing out as dreamt at one of my many office jobs. Quinn, Olga, Deshunda, Jane, and even me, among countless others, we'd all experienced psychic phenomena in addition to the nighttime intrusions with which we've been plagued.

Psychic phenomena are something that will continue to surface in many of these stories, especially the ones in which the beings—whatever they are—seem to be keeping an eye on people.

For Deshunda, a predisposition towards psychic experiences wasn't the only thing she shared with her mother, and whatever was happening to them had a disturbing physical element.

"There were days I would wake up with bruises on my arms. I don't remember how I got them. It looked like three claws, like somebody had scratched me, like I was fighting something," she said. "I remember this clearly, [my mother] said to me, 'I used to wake up with those same marks on me.'"

Those marks might be explained by another experience related to me by Deshunda.

This event, she said, took place at her childhood home in Joliet, Illinois, in 1987 when she was 12 years old.

"[The house where] we stayed at the time was in the country," she said. "There was a barn there, and some nearby houses. They've built a lot there now, but at the time there were a lot of fields, and we had a big backyard."

I had to stay late for detention after school one day. I remember going into the house after I came home, thinking I was going to be in trouble. But nobody was home. I had to go through the garage to get into the house, and I saw the car was there, so I didn't understand where everybody was at.

So, I started calling, "Momma! Momma!"

And I called for my sisters, but nobody answered. Just then the phone rang, and I went to go pick it up.

A robotic voice said to me, "Little girl, is your mommy or daddy home?"

I dropped the phone. The minute I dropped it, I felt sick. I felt drowsy and sleepy, and I had a headache. I laid down in the bunk bed in our room, and it was like I could not move.

I saw four little things come in the room, they were suited up—it was like a skintight, blue, protective suit—they were bald, with big, black eyes and really not much of a nose or mouth, and all I can remember is being paralyzed with fear. I was trying to fight it; I was trying to move.

Two were on either side of me, and they weren't touching me. It was like I was levitated. I was looking at one of these things straight in its eyes, and I'm trying to fight it and I can't move. That's all I can remember.

She later asked her sister where they were that day but said that her sister maintains she "doesn't know what I'm talking about."

Deshunda never watched much science fiction or absorbed similar media as a child, and it wasn't until her twenties that she started seeing representations of the beings she encountered that day.

"It's never left my mind, and I wonder if that's why I'm so into this stuff now," she said. "I see people talking about it, and I think 'That's what I saw! That's what came in the room.'"

When I asked if she'd had any bedroom visitations since the one in 2007, Deshunda replied, "I have not, and I pray to God I don't again."

There's one more strange tale to be told before we move on to the next chapter, one separated from the others only slightly in that this witness didn't report any of the same psychic phenomena, although there are other parapsychological similarities.

24-year-old Lauren Nevil of Farmington, New York, contacted us in January of 2021 to report a sighting of strange, white aerial lights seen during a power outage the previous November.

The outage came as the result of a stormfront with high winds which knocked out power for thousands of residents in western New York on November 15th, 2020.

During our interview, Lauren said she was preparing to go to bed that evening when her mother alerted her to something strange happening outside.

"I remember specifically because I was trying to get to sleep, and it was a windy night, and all the power went out. I live in a townhouse complex. I remember the power going out and my mom came upstairs [calling my name]. I said, 'What? I'm trying to go to sleep because I have to get up for work the next morning.' She said, 'Look outside!' She was freaking out," said Lauren.

"I looked out my bedroom window, facing towards the parking lot, and I saw all of these strange lights in the sky," she continued. "My mom was flipping out, and I was like 'What is going on?' She called my sister into my room, and we could see everything because there was no light pollution, so it was clear. It was a clear sky. We didn't know what was going on. We didn't know if it was satellites. My sister counted 10 to 15 lights. I'm not sure how long it lasted, maybe about 10 to 15 minutes."

Historical weather data for that evening showed that at the time of the sighting, which Lauren believed took place between 10 and 10:30 p.m., the sky over Farmington was mostly cloudy, meaning that while a small portion of the sky might have been visible, it would have been mostly obscured.

"It was just a bunch [of lights] all clustered together," she explained. "They were bright, [and] they were just sitting there. I think the oddest thing was that they were clustered together in a group—not in any sort of formation. It was very strange."

Weather conditions that evening make it likely that the lights were below the cloud cover, given Lauren's description of events.

"This wasn't like any star or anything," she said of the lights.

After the three women spent "10 to 15 minutes" observing the stationary lights, they "all just kind of disappeared."

"[The lights disappeared] kind of like one at a time," she said.

Lauren told me that she had done some research of her own prior to contacting us at the Singular Fortean Society.

"I've looked up websites where people report UFOs, and in the area that I live people have seen stuff, although that's the first time I've ever really seen anything," she said. "I'm kind of freaked out."

After doing a little research of my own, I found five reported sightings from Farmington in the case files of the National UFO Reporting Center (NUFORC).

NUFORC's files also showed that the city of Rochester, only 20 miles northwest of Farmington and located directly adjacent to Lake Ontario, has had many dozens of reported UFO sightings going back decades.

This sighting wasn't the only unusual encounter had by Lauren, either, who said she and her sister have also experienced a string of nighttime visitations by unknown entities.

"When we used to live in our old house, before we moved, my sister and I would sometimes feel like someone was sitting on our bed, like the pressure. It felt like someone was sitting there. That happened every once in a while," she said. "Our beds would shake, too. We don't know what that was."

Her sister, said Lauren, had even woken up to find "someone

was standing over her, leaning over to look at her," although "that hasn't happened in a long time."

Lauren said that, despite having been in bed when she experienced the paranormal events, she was sure that she was "fully awake" at the times they occurred.

There's something deeply unsettling about these experiences. They are violations of one's health, bodily autonomy, and even sanity, but beyond all of that, there is the deeper mystery of their commonality; the real, esoteric truth staring out at us from behind a patchwork curtain of many seemingly disparate phenomena.

What is it that these strange visitors are after? To observe people who experience psychic phenomena? Or is that simply sometimes a byproduct of the intrusions, our mind's natural reaction to the assault on our consciousness? Perhaps some psychic sensitivity means we're more capable of having the experiences in the first place. Or is it completely unrelated, just another coincidence in a lifetime of coincidences that we attempt to put together like pieces from several different jigsaw puzzles?

I'd say time will tell, but I don't know that. So, I'll say time might tell, but then again, it might not.

CHAPTER 4

A MATTER OF PERSPECTIVE

It would be disingenuous to pretend that no aspect of these accounts differentiates them, although as often as not, it's the witness's reaction that separates the narratives. Not everyone reacts the same way to the things they find in the night. After all, sometimes it really is just a matter of perspective.

I spoke to a woman in July of 2020 who told me that in her early teen years she'd seen a "gargoyle" with feathered wings perched on the roof of her family's home.

She said that her sighting took place in 2002 in Babcock, Wisconsin—an unincorporated town of around 125 people which lies about 120 miles west of Lake Michigan.

This sighting report was initially given to Lon Strickler of Phantoms & Monsters before being further investigated by me, and details of Lon's investigation have been used to fully develop the account. It should be noted that the woman's account as told to me was consistent with what was told to Lon.

"It was summer; I don't remember which month," the witness said to me during our interview. "I'm a night owl, so I was up fairly late; it couldn't have been too late, maybe around midnight or so. I was watching TV in my room—my room is on the second floor of the house—and right outside my bedroom window I had access to the roof of the living room. I was watching TV one night and I decided I was going to lie down instead of just sit on my bed, and as I was adjusting to lie down, I noticed something really weird on the corner of the roof. My bed was positioned right up against the wall where the window was, so the end of my bed was right up against the window. I had a pretty good view of at least half the roof to the living room."

Due to some previous issues, we had a security light installed in our backyard, so that lit up the whole backyard and the roof that

I could see. I noticed this weird thing, and I'm kind of looking, and it honestly made me think of a gargoyle, except for the wings just didn't look right. The wings had feathers—and they were really, really perfect feathers—they were a light grey color, they were a little lighter grey than the skin of the thing.

I couldn't see its face at all, I basically just had a side view of it because it was facing out towards my backyard and the top of the wings kind of blocked off the face. I couldn't tell if there was an ear or eyes or anything. I could tell it had a bald head and it had, at least from what I could tell from the back, it looked like a pretty normal, human-type neck. I could also see from the side view that it had human-shaped legs, because it was kind of perched on my roof with its knees bent and its feet on the roof. I couldn't see its arms or anything.

I'm guessing the arms and the hands were just positioned between the legs, and the hands were on top of the roof. The feet looked fairly human-like, too. It was just really weird looking. I've never seen anything like that. There were no scales on the skin, it just looked like regular skin, just grey. The only part that had feathers were the wings, and they kind of had an angel wing shape to them. I would guess, I'm like 5'2", even at that time I was like 5'2", and had it been standing up it probably would have been at least a couple of feet taller than me.

I watched it for probably close to a half hour, and I kind of got bored because it wasn't doing anything. It didn't move, it didn't make noise. I mean, just nothing. Then I went back to my movie and fell asleep.

I didn't feel like it was a threat to me. I just seemed more surprised than anything, because you don't expect to see something like that.

In her interview with Lon, the woman added that she had "made an attempt to get its attention, softly speaking to it, but the being never responded."

When she woke up around sunrise the next day—sometime between 5 and 6 a.m.—she checked the roof, but the being had gone.

At that time, she heard a "really weird, high-pitched radio frequency sound."

"I couldn't pinpoint where it was coming from, it just sounded like it was all around," she said of the sound. "I thought about asking people about it, but then I backed away from that because you know how people can be. I don't know if anyone else heard it. I know my parents didn't, neither did my siblings. It was just me that heard it, because they weren't early risers at that time, either."

The Sandhill State Wildlife Area is within a few miles of the sighting area, and the woman said she remembers hearing strange reports over her dad's scanner from Department of Natural Resources (DNR) personnel who would mention "hybrids of certain animals."

"This is probably going to sound even crazier," she said. "I don't remember when this happened, but my dad, he used to have a scanner for when the weather would get bad. He had the channel for the DNR, and occasionally some of the guys talking on the scanner late at night would mention hybrids of certain animals, but they wouldn't say what. I don't know if any of that is related [to my sighting]. It's just really weird. As far as I know, I don't know if anyone has ever seen anything like I did."

Like many witnesses, she said that she's largely kept her story to herself.

"I've only told a handful of people that I'm really close with, because I know they won't think I'm nuts," she explained. "Pretty much my entire life I've dealt with paranormal experiences, but that one definitely takes the cake of strange things."

As for the creature itself, she's not sure what she witnessed, although she has done some research.

"The only thing that really confused me about it, and I've researched quite a few reports of Mothman sightings, was that people tend to report that you feel a lot of dread with the sighting," she said. "That's what threw me off. I wasn't sure if I was seeing Mothman, because people say it's associated with dread and then something bad happens. But nothing bad happened after that sighting."

The world first heard of the Mothman in November of 1966, when a series of sightings of a large, black, flying creature with glowing red eyes took place in and around Point Pleasant, West Virginia. The sightings purportedly culminated in the collapse of the Silver Bridge spanning the Ohio River between Point Pleasant and Gallipolis, Ohio on December 15th, 1967, and to this day there are some that maintain the creature's appearance was a portent to the disaster. Although to some Mothman was an aberrant phenomenon, similar to the Flatwoods Monster or Kelly-Hopkinsville Goblins, sightings of similar creatures, especially along the Ohio River Valley and in the region surrounding Lake Michigan, point to a more widespread phenomenon. This has led to the association of a variety of qualities to Mothman, including fear and portending doom, and supports the idea that there may be more than one entity behind the sightings.

I took the opportunity to explain that, although fear is a commonly reported element, it's not reported by every witness, and perhaps in this case that could be because she didn't seem to have the creature's attention, nor did she see the glowing eyes that disturb so many who view them. Or, perhaps, it simply hadn't wanted to scare her. People react differently to events, too, and there's really no way of knowing at this point why she wasn't afraid, we can only note that she was not.

Also, I said, the idea that 'Mothman' or other flying creature sightings portend disasters is often refuted by researchers who believe that the infamous collapse of the Silver Bridge acted only as a convenient narrative ending to the story being told by author John Keel and was not, in fact, related to the Mothman phenomenon. In fact, sightings of winged humanoids around Point Pleasant and along the Ohio River Valley never really ended after the event, a very inconvenient truth for those attempting to connect that particular disaster to the phenomenon.

Keel, the man most famous for investigating sightings of the Mothman in Point Pleasant, was an excellent storyteller; one who never let the truth get in the way of a good story. The tragedy of the Silver Bridge collapse served as a tidy ending to the narrative of his book The Mothman Prophecies, but actual evidence of any connection between that event and sightings of winged humanoids is nonexistent. There are few things, however, that an audience loves more than a tidy narrative, and so the legend persists to this day.

That narrative was later reinforced when the 2002 movie adaptation of his book added even more, entirely fictional, events involving winged humanoids and disasters, including a connection to the devastating hurricane of 1900 in Galveston, Texas, and the infamous 1986 meltdown of a nuclear reactor in Chernobyl Nuclear Power Plant, near the city of Pripyat in the north of the Ukrainian SSR. Neither of those events had any sightings of winged humanoids associated with them prior to the movie, and yet, a quick Google search can find plenty of people who swear by the existence of "the Black Bird of Chernobyl."

"I always wondered about that," she responded. "That would be a little too crazy."

Ultimately, said the woman, "I always figured it was one of those creatures that hadn't been discovered, just kind of doing its thing and not realizing the effect it's having on people."

That opinion resonated with me. My own experiences tended to support the idea that whatever these things were, they were merely going about their business, regardless of what we thought of it.

This certainly seemed to be the case with a woman who said she and her husband saw an "unknown flying human owl" perched in a tree near their apartment in Hoffman Estates, Illinois, towards the end of October 2019.

The original report was sent as an email to The Singular Fortean Society.

I am writing to you today in regard to the Mothman/Human Owl. This is Diana and Jesus G. So, we live at The Reserve in Hoffman Estates, and our apartment complex is next to an empty corn field and across from Barrington there is a forest preserve. My husband and I live on the third floor of the complex as we face another building but can also see towards the corn field to our right. We also have lots of trees around our building almost as tall as the building itself.

We would normally go out to our porch every night to smoke a cigarette, and about a month and two weeks ago [in late October 2019], we went out at about 9 or 10 p.m. We usually leave our phones inside so we can enjoy [a] little chat and gaze at the stars, or even see a pack of coyotes roaming around the streets and apartments, or sometimes even head back into the field towards the forest (keep in mind this field has no crop so it is empty, and you can see towards the street).

Well, that specific night my husband was to my right, and he is taller than me, so I was talking to him taking a puff, when I noticed something in the pine tree (I believe it is pine) behind him; right at the top of the tree, not in between the branches or nothing, RIGHT AT THE TOP. He noticed I wasn't paying attention, so he turned around to look, and sure enough there was what we thought was a huge owl looking out towards the field then looking back around. So, after a couple seconds, maybe 30 seconds, we started to question each other.

"What is that?"

"Is that an owl?"

I'm talking about this thing was pitch black, but its wings and shape were HUGE, as you can see that from the reflection of the sky which was lighter. I recall continuing to smoke as we tried to examine this creature looking around. Once we had noticed it, I don't recall 'it' ever looking at us.

We were already a few minutes outside before I noticed, so I'm not sure if he ever looked down at us. I was more into the body shape though, I could see huge, long, black wings. We couldn't really see any details as it was super dark.

My husband was trying to get closer to the edge to get a good look at it, but we could really just see the long wings and huge shape.

Well, after finishing our square, we said, "Yeah it might just be an owl, a pretty big one for sure," and we came inside our complex which is the roof of the building.

Normally at night we could hear the animals climbing on the rails and roof, but our roommate whose room is next to the porch, he states he always hears something walking at night by his window or above it. I'm not sure if it's that creature, the tree is right next to us so he can easily climb onto the building.

Jesus and I never saw it again when we would go out there, but we did joke around about it being behind us on the roof and that it would pick us up and fly away; he did it to scare me. We thought nothing of it until we read the article about a semi-truck driver who spotted something similar at O'Hare Airport, which is not far from here. Once we saw that we just stared at each other because we recall what we saw, so we now know WE WEREN'T SEEING THINGS, LIKE THIS WAS LEGIT. We sometimes step out for a moment to see if we find it again, but so far, he's been gone...and that's our story about seeing this unknown flying human owl.

That report from O'Hare is discussed later in the book, but suffice it to say, for now at least, that it's another example of these reports creating this cascading effect of other experiences being reported.

In this case, I followed up with Diana via email.

"The thing is, we could see the black shadow of it holding on to the tree, but not the exact tip of the tree," she said in response to a series of questions I sent her. "There were no more branches above him, so it could have been he was perched. We tried comparing it to an eagle, but even a humongous eagle wouldn't compare to it. It has to be twice or maybe three times the size. We'd say about six to eight feet tall, genuinely not lying about how huge it looked."

"We were just smoking relaxing before hitting the pillow for a night's rest, clear mind," Diana added. "Actually, me and my husband were talking about a family issue, and the very next way we received some bad news."

Diana also reported having had paranormal experiences in the past but said they have not increased in frequency since the sighting.

"I usually have a lot of paranormal activity happen to me, but not any different since [the sighting]," she said.

"For as long as I can remember, I've always experienced something," Diana continued. "Usually, I would experience sleep paralysis, and many times I've been woken up to someone standing over my bed watching me. As much as a little girl, an old lady which I believe is my grandma, an older man, one who's cuddled me and also one who's left me scratches on my body. I've had someone wake me from my sleep at 4 a.m. and walk out of my room into the same empty house, and when I got up to look around nobody was there."

"I've had so many experiences," she said. "It's never ending for me."

Such is the experience of so many of the witnesses to the impossible whose accounts are shared in this work.

CHAPTER 5

WATCH WHERE YOU WALK

So much of what these witnesses have described feels like observation to me; strange entities peering around corners and leaning over beds, staring at us when we're most vulnerable. But almost as much seems coincidental, an interruption that is perhaps as jarring to the otherworldly entities involved as it is to the human beings who have blundered into them. It's as though another, invisible world is layered over our own, one in which exists a vast ecology of things not yet understood by humanity. Things which sometimes, at their leisure, observe us for their own unintelligible reasons, but also which, due to the whims of fate, are sometimes themselves observed by us while going about their weird business.

The seemingly accidental nature of these experiences, however, makes them no less terrifying to many of the witnesses subjected to them.

The Singular Fortean Society received an email in July of 2019 by a man named Mike who said that in September of 2003 he had seen a flying humanoid in a wooded area on the southern edge of Springfield, Illinois.

I had contact with a flying humanoid in September 2003. It was in Springfield, Illinois, in the woods behind the [now defunct] Four Seasons bar. I was walking down the railroad tracks around 10:30 p.m., when someone in a house along the tracks picked up the phone. I got spooked they were calling the cops. So, I went into the woods. I waited about 30 minutes and figured that they did not call the cops (walking on tracks is a crime), so I decided to leave the woods and follow the tracks home like I have done many times before.

I got about 50 feet from where I had spent the last 30 minutes, and I heard footsteps coming towards me in the leaves. I know what human footsteps sound like in the woods. Fearing an encounter with a homeless person, I hid behind a tree that was right there; the steps stopped right on the other side of the tree. I waited a couple minutes and figured they went towards the way out.

I decided to go back, where I waited for the 30 minutes. About five minutes later, I had the worst feeling, like I was not supposed to be where I was and to get out of these woods right now. I ran fast for about four blocks, [and] when I got to the outskirts of the woods the small trees started acting funny, kind of spinning in circles on the top; for some reason it almost felt like the woods were alive and the trees were going to grab me.

All of a sudden, all the hair stood up on the back of my neck and I felt pure evil behind me. Something told me don't look back you're not going to like what you see. So, I looked back and saw a creature on what appeared to be a flying scooter of some kind, flying over the treetops parallel to the way I was going, perfectly silent. I ran like hell and didn't look back. Several months later, I read an article in a magazine about strange creatures, and the picture of the "flying humanoid " looked exactly like what I saw.

It wasn't until mid-August that I was able to speak with Mike over the phone.

"It's really got me stumped," he said. "I remember the details pretty good. I know the trails real good, I grew up in that area. I used to ride my bike on the dirt trails there as a kid. I pretty much knew the trail like the back of my hand; I knew exactly where it happened at. I knew the trail that I heard the thing walking down, and there was some light, it wasn't pitch black. It was the end of September, so a lot of the leaves were on the ground. There was some light coming through the trees, I could still see."

Especially puzzling to Mike was the missing tree.

"That tree, there was no sign of a tree ever being there that I hid behind. It was on top of a ravine, there were no roots. Right off one side of the trail is [the] ravine. And right where the tree was it almost would have been in the middle of the trail, but when I stepped back behind the tree, I was standing flat-footed on the ground." he explained. "It was weird that I remember hiding behind that tree, but there was no actual tree there. It was almost like it had been an implanted memory or something. I wonder if it actually might have been aliens or something like that."

But that wasn't the only aspect of high strangeness present in the report. The phantom footsteps remain unexplained, as does the intense fear he felt even prior to his sighting—not to mention the appearance of the creature itself.

"I assumed [whoever was making the footsteps I heard] was a homeless guy," Mike said. "I had a stick and I'm behind the tree and I'm waiting. I was by myself; I didn't have a phone on me. I figured if he tried something I'm going to fight with him. So, I hid behind the tree, and I heard the footsteps, and they stopped right on the other side of the tree, where the trail was. The trail I was on was a little 'off trail,' one [people] don't ride their motorcycles on, so it had a lot of leaves on it, but the main trail didn't have a lot of leaves because there's a lot of motorcycle riders that go back there. When it got to the trail, I waited a couple of minutes, and I figured that whoever it was went towards the [way out of the woods].

"I went back about 50 feet or so, and I smoked another cigarette, and a couple minutes later, that's when I had that bad feeling," he continued. "The feeling just overwhelmed me; it was like 'What are you doing? You're not supposed to be here. Matter of fact, get the hell out of here, right now.' That's when I ran out of the woods. I ran as fast as I could for three or four blocks."

"The area behind these woods, I remember when I was a kid, there used to be little structures built, like little wood structures, down in the ravine, and we never saw any homeless people back there," added Mike.

The trail exited into a "circle track" of cleared land where people would sometimes ride motorcycles, and as he left the woods, "the trees seemed like they were spinning in circles around the top, and I felt like the trees were going to grab me, like they were alive, like the whole woods were alive."

And that's when Mike felt his final pang of terror that night.

"All of a sudden, all of the hair on the back of my neck stood up and something said, 'Whatever you do, don't look behind you, because you're not going to like what you see.' I looked behind me and I saw that thing flying parallel to me," he said. "It looked like it was wrapped in something, like it maybe had a cape on—it had something wrapped around it. It looked like a person, like a big person, on a scooter; I swear I could almost see the handlebars on the thing. That's what my recollection was. A scooter, with no wheels, with some big guy, probably six foot, 250 pounds or something like that. It looked like a little Honda scooter, and it looked like it had a little light on one side of it. I remember seeing something shining, like on the front of it—kind of like a headlight."

Whatever the flying humanoid wanted, Mike wasn't about to find out, and again he ran, this time to the relative safety of the well-lit suburban streets.

"I went back a few months later, during the daytime of course, I don't think I'd go back in those woods at night. I don't know if whatever was there lives there, or if it was just travelling through, but I don't think I would go back there at night," he said. "I'm glad I got out of those woods."

That "flying humanoid" Mike had seen in a magazine was a still image from the June 17th, 2005, video shot by Horacio Roquet after leaving his apartment in Unidad Habitacional Lomas de Platero, Mexico City, at 7 a.m. to go to work. The video itself is a shaky, hand-shot affair showing a roughly humanoid object with what may be a light on it floating in the sky. Its only source is rense.com, a far right, blatantly racist conspiracy site that advertises books like The Myth of German Villainy and propagates dangerous misinformation about everything from the environment to medical science—the site is everything we should be ashamed of in this industry.

The report published to this paranormal embarrassment is analogous to the one I received from Mike, in that Roquet seems to have encountered the phenomenon represented within it entirely by accident. He was reportedly unsettled by the experience and felt "very nervous" while viewing the object.

"It looked like a human-shaped body, 'standing' vertical and just floating over the roof. I was shocked. The figure was not facing me...I was looking straight at its right side. It was tall. No sound was heard, and we both stood still, watching, while I continued recording," Roquet said. "Then the dark body started moving to the right slowly and rose several feet in the sky and then hovered again, completely still. I kept recording all the time. I was very nervous, trying to control myself, and I taped the thing the best I could. After several minutes the dark figure moved again to the left, disappearing behind the building's roof. The sighting lasted about ten minutes."

"I don't have any clue what this weird thing was," he added.

None of us do.

Pockets of nature nestled within otherwise urban environments seem as popular a place as any to experience the impossible. Many of the sightings we'll examine take place within or directly adjacent to these juxtaposed spaces. Often present, too, is some aspect of liminality; a transition between two places or states of being. For some of those cases we examined earlier, that liminal space was the bridge between awake and dreaming, but for Mike, and the similar cases we are about to peruse, it is travel.

Riverview Park was an amusement park on the shore of the North Branch of the Chicago River from 1904 to 1967, when it was bought by an investment firm and demolished without warning. It was gone by the time David Ramos had his encounter with a red-eyed, winged man in 1971, but it was a popular enough landmark, and when I was asked to visit Chicago in February of 2020 to film a documentary about the Lake Michigan Mothman for German public television, it was easy enough to find out what had been built on the old park's bones.

From there, the director of the documentary, Ole, and I found the approximate area where David had his sighting. There was still a path lined with trees, although they stood naked in the frigid February air, and looking down the embankment, I could see where perhaps David's friends had so carefreely thrown around rubble while he waited cautiously on the path. That same caution which, ironically, led him face-to-face with a living nightmare.

In December of 2019, I was contacted by David, a 60-year-old retired police officer who said that at the age of 12, he had encountered a shadowy, winged humanoid near the North Branch of the Chicago River.

David served as a police officer in Chicago's 14th district from 1994-2009.

When I was a kid about 12 years old in Chicago, we used to live near old Riverview Park. A bunch of us boys were playing around near the banks of the [North Branch of the Chicago River], throwing rubble concrete from when they demolished the park into the river and making big splashes. I didn't like being too close to the water, so while the others were down by the riverbank, I went up to the path again by myself.

I looked northward and I swear I saw a very tall, skinny man [who was] very dark on the path about 200 feet away. He glanced my way and threw his arms up, and he had wings and ran and flapped them and disappeared into the trees towards the bank. I was petrified right there...and looked around but my friends were looking south and still playing around. I said, "Did you guys see that guy?" I wasn't sure If I was seeing a guy pranking [us] or what.

It was always spooky by the river, even in broad daylight, where they demolished Riverview. I tried to explain but [my friends] told me to shut up and didn't pay any attention to me, [since] I was smaller and younger than them. I am now 60 years old [and] a retired Chicago police officer living in Florida, and [I] never told anybody else really until I saw your article just now. And it shocked the shit out of me. I too got the feeling of something evil that day and wanted to go home immediately.

In a follow-up email he added additional details.

I tried to get a look at his face when he glanced my way. Back then I thought he had like a scary Halloween mask on or something. There was no focal point for me because it was not a human-type face. Big eyes were the thing I remember. It still creeps me out to this day.

I tried to remember if something bad happened to any of us shortly after that and...I just remembered that one of the older boys that we were with that day shot and killed a rival gang member shortly after that sighting. He was 16 at the time and went to jail at 17 for at least five years for murder.

As previously noted, I had always found the arguments in favor of winged humanoids as harbingers of doom to be weak. Terrible things happen every day with no winged humanoids around to telegraph them, and we've personally received a multitude of such cases here at The Singular Fortean Society which didn't lead to any disaster for anybody. But it's a popular narrative, so the idea continues to pop up in these kinds of cases.

Not long after exchanging emails with David, I was able to interview him over the phone. He'd since moved from Illinois to Florida, but he was happy to revisit his experience with me.

"There was a path above the water, about five feet above the water on a slope. I wasn't too comfortable being down there with these guys throwing concrete all over the place. I thought it was pretty dangerous, so I went up the embankment to the path," said David.

"It was a fall day. In Chicago it's always very gray, not too sunny or anything like that, but it was still daytime," he continued. "I was by myself [on the path], and I looked down there, and there was a tall, black figure walking. He looked like he had a cape on. He was north of me, about two hundred feet. He was like a big, tall man with a cape on. He looked seven feet tall. He was facing north, [away from me]. I don't know if he sensed me or whatever, but he looked back in my direction, and I just couldn't make out a face. I was like, 'Where's his face?' I couldn't make out a face, but I noticed he had big eyes—like he had goggles on or something—they were yellowish red. He threw up his right hand and there was a wing. It was huge! He ran north a few steps, started beating his wings, and went up into the trees."

"I was looking for a regular face, but it didn't have a face—or it was too dark to see it. But it looked like he had goggles on; I couldn't explain that," David added. "I was expecting this thing to be a man, but it turned around and it wasn't a man."

The experience had a profound effect on David that he's carried with him for nearly 50 years.

"I never went back again," he said. "They built one of our stations right over there, the 19th district, that's where we used to exchange our cars and have our cars serviced. Even as a policeman, going over there for that, I still remembered that day and it was very creepy. It stuck with me forever."

Several months after filming the documentary, I received an email from 79-year-old Gerald Turrise. He wanted to recount an experience he'd had with a weird, winged creature in Illinois during the winter of 1957.

"I realize this story is a little late, but I never knew who to tell my story to until I came across [your article] about the man who saw a birdman at O'Hare airport," Gerald wrote in his email. "I'm 79 years old now and this happened a long time ago. It was around 1957 when I was with my late brother Gene and his late brother-in law, we were hunting in the Braidwood, Illinois area for pheasants and rabbits. As we were walking in this large open field, there was a lone, large tree standing in the middle of the field. When we were directly under it, a huge man-sized creature sailed over our heads into the woods across the road. We were stunned, we just looked at each other too dumbfounded to speak."

I wrote back to Gerald and asked for any additional details he could remember.

"I was a young teenager at the time, and it was early wintertime, [the time of day] was mid-morning," he responded. "The winged creature had the body of a large man with legs, but it was covered over the whole body with dark, tan-colored feathers. This happened so long ago I don't recall what the face looked like. I'm glad to tell this story to someone who has knowledge of such creatures before I die."

Now, I have a habit of asking people if they've ever had any other experiences that they'd describe as unusual, and there's a good reason for it. As often as not, it leads me to something like Gerald's subsequent admission that he'd "had an encounter at a U.S. Army station at a Nike Hercules missile site in Northfield, Illinois" in 1963.

"I was on guard duty at the time at our radar station," he said. "It was after midnight when I witnessed a UFO in the sky southeast of my location, maybe a mile away around 1,000 feet above the terrain. I watched it for a few minutes before I made a phone call to our command offices in Arlington, Illinois, to report what I was observing. I was contacted a few days later by Dr. J. Allen Hynek. This report is documented in project Blue Book. Dr. Hynek had told me he was informed to tell me that what I saw was just a private airplane towing an advertising sign. I doubt they would be flying at that time of night, Now, there's no way a plane could ever make the moves I witnessed, and at the end of the encounter this UFO just shot up into space as fast as a bullet."

Gerald described the UFO as "saucer-shaped" with rotating lights that encircled the craft illuminating what looked like windows.

"[The size was] difficult to know exactly, but I'd say about 100 feet in diameter," he said.

The craft's color, he added, was indiscernible because it was nighttime.

A review of the Project Blue Book case files confirmed the date of Gerald's sighting as May 11th, 1963, and the official evaluation as "aircraft."

In further correspondence with me, Gerald explained that the impression he got was that Dr. Hynek was being pressured into unfairly discrediting his sighting.

A few days after his sighting, he said, someone claiming to be Dr. J. Allen Hynek called him on the phone.

"Well, it was, I think, days later—let's not forget 57 years have

A photo of Gerald Turrise from his time in the military.

IMAGE CREDIT: Gerald Turrise

1 - 31 MAY 1963 SIGHTINGS

DATE	LOCATION	OBSERVER	EVALUATION
1	Silver Grove, Kentucky	Garlinger	Other (UNRELIABLE REPORT)
3	29.57N 140 03W (Pacific)	Military	BALLOON
4	Ocean City, Maryland	Sloanacker	AIRCRAFT
5	Arlington Heights, Illinois	Sonnenberg	BALLOON
6	Whiteman AFB, Missouri	Military	BALLOON
8	North Vernon, Indiana	Civilian (PHYSICAL SPECIMEN)	Other (ASD TEST VEHICLE W/PARACHUTE)
8	58.15N 169.20N (Pacific)	Military	AIRCRAFT
11	Northfield, Illinois	Turrise	AIRCRAFT
15	Louisiana-Mississippi Area	Multiple	Other (ROCKET LAUNCH)
15	Beaufort, South Carolina	Wolfe	AIRCRAFT
15	Evanston, Illinois	Henkin	AIRCRAFT
17	46.13N 173.53W (Pacific)	Military	Other (FLARE)
	46.15N 171.15W (Pacific)	Military	Astro (METEOR)
	New Plymouth, New Zealand	Chapman	UNIDENTIFIED
21	40.02N 10.16E (Atlantic)	Military	Other (MISSILE/ROCKET)
22	Parkersburg, West Virginia	Mackey	Astro (METEOR)
22	Pequannock, New Jersey	Jackson	UNIDENTIFIED
22	43.20N 172.50W (Pacific)	Military	Astro (METEOR)
24	Haleiwa, Oahu, Hawaii	Military	INSUFFICIENT DATA
26	Gulf of Mexico	Military	INSUFFICIENT DATA
28	Philadelphia, Pennsylvania	Civilian	Other (CONTRAILS)
29	30.50N 169.00W (Pacific)	Military	INSUFFICIENT DATA
31	44N 49W (Atlantic)	Military	Other (ELECTRONIC INTERFERENCE FROM WITHIN AIRCRAFT)

An excerpt from Project Blue Book's May 1963 case listing, which shows Turrise's sighting.

passed—and it was late at night," he said.

> I was asleep and the phone woke me. The man [on the other end] introduced himself as Dr. J. Allen Hynek and went on to give me his message that [he said] was relayed to him. He went on to say that he was told to tell me what I witnessed was a small private airplane that was flying over the area, and the plane was towing a sign behind it at around the time of [my sighting].
>
> He concluded with these words, "This is what I was told to tell you." I went on to say that there was no airplane that could maneuver the way this UFO was doing, up and down, side to side, and coming to a complete stop. [There were] lights that completely circled the craft that were rotating, displaying what looked like windows, and the most shocking part of the whole episode was when it departed, the craft looked like it got shot out of a cannon.
>
> I mean to tell you I was a radar operator at a Nike Hercules missile site, and I've witnessed missile firings, and this UFO took off into space faster than the missiles I've seen being launched. He ended with this: "I'm sorry, this was all I was to say to you, good night."
>
> That was all I can recollect from the past of my account of the incident.

The missile site at which Gerald was stationed—which was active from 1955 to 1974—is just south of Chicago. Braidwood, where he had his winged creature sighting, is approximately 70 miles southwest of the site.

Dr. Hynek was a scientist and UFO investigator who was initially skeptical of the phenomenon when he signed on as a scientific consultant to the United States Air Force's Project Sign in 1948, but his opinion on the quality of evidence in favor of UFOs gradually shifted as he worked on projects like Sign and Blue Book.

He quickly grew frustrated with how flippantly his fellow scientists treated UFOs.

"Ridicule is not part of the scientific method, and people should not be taught that it is," Dr. Hynek wrote in an article for the April 1953 issue of the Journal of the Optical Society of America titled 'Unusual Aerial Phenomena.' "The steady flow of reports, often made in concert by reliable observers, raises questions of scientific obligation and responsibility. Is there...any residue that is worthy of scientific attention? Or, if there isn't, does not an obligation exist to say so to the public—not in words of open ridicule but seriously, to keep faith with the trust the public places in science and scientists?"

Dr. Hynek went on to eventually found the Center for UFO Studies (CUFOS) in 1973, and even presented a statement on UFOs to the United Nations General Assembly in 1978.

He remained a leader in the field of ufology until his death in 1986.

Dr. Hynek resented what he saw as Project Blue Book's mandate to debunk UFOs, and while it's not known who exactly might have told him to discredit Gerald's sighting, doing so would be consistent with the perceived aims of the project. It's entirely possible that, since Dr. Hynek's specialty was in astronomy, someone within the Air Force disingenuously identified the object as an airplane and ordered him to report it as such to Gerald, despite any evidence to the contrary.

The sighting location itself could have even played a role, considering its sensitive nature. The Air Force may have been loath to report an unidentified flying object so close to a Nike Hercules missile site.

Also of interest are the themes present in Gerald's encounters, the ones we keep seeing repeatedly throughout these tales, not just of travel, but of observation. Although in this case, if the UFO was observing Gerald, he certainly returned the favor.

Travel and observation were both key elements in the experience of a woman who had emailed The Singular Fortean Society in January of 2020. She asked that she be referred to only as Kel.

My roommate got a dog, and I was helping by taking him out to go to the bathroom, in the Albany Park neighborhood in Chicago. I was also going to go for a long walk because the dog was restless.

As I started to walk down the sidewalk, I looked down the sidewalk ahead of me. Then I saw a very tall, skinny, all-black figure about seven to eight feet tall. It was shuffling towards me very slowly. I stopped and stared, trying to convince myself it was a person, but I could not make out any arms, or it's as if it had long arms being tucked behind itself. I couldn't make out a round head shape either.

I instantly got scared. I didn't have a good feeling. I got creeped out and fled back to my apartment, looking over my shoulder it was still there. I just wanted to tell someone. I am not sure what I just saw but it was unsettling.

Kel reported that she "looked at it for about [a] minute," but "couldn't make out what it was, and got a very unsettling feeling about the tall dark figure shuffling slowly towards [her]."

At that point, she "pulled the dog along and ran in the direction of [her] apartment."

"I glanced over my shoulder [two times] to see if it was still there, and the figure was walking slowly in my direction. Not aggressively coming towards me, but it was facing me, watching me, and I got an eerie feeling that I should get back inside," said Kel.

I asked Kel to describe the figure in more detail, if possible.

"[It was] definitely a humanoid solid shadow figure," she said. "It wasn't transparent or anything. Just black, skinny and very tall, and it had weight to it as it shuffled. I could not see eyes, or a face, the head was not a round silhouette. I saw two legs, like I could not make out any pants or shoes. No clothes. No arms dangling at the torso sides, but there appeared to be something being tucked away behind them. Just a dark black solid figure."

According to Kel, "The figure was under the streetlamp on St. Louis [Avenue] and Sunnyside [Avenue] in Chicago, on the northwest side of the St. Louis sidewalk just across Sunnyside. I was on the southwest side of the St. Louis sidewalk on the other side of Sunnyside."

"I was very confused why I could not see clothes or features besides a missized head and two legs and no arms, or some arms or something tucked behind the figure, just black," she added. "I feel like the figure should have been better illuminated because it was right underneath the streetlamp light."

Kel told me that while she had experienced a couple of paranormal events in the past and was perhaps sometimes privy to psychic intuitions, she'd "never had any experiences with physically seeing UFOs or otherworldly apparitions, not even ghosts."

"Definitely felt nuts after seeing this one though," she said.

I didn't blame her. That seems to be the general consensus, after all.

CHAPTER 6

HIGH STRANGENESS ON THE HYPNOSIS HIGHWAY

Few activities are more adept at initiating an altered state of consciousness than driving. It happens so frequently, in fact, that we've come up with a phrase specifically to describe it: highway hypnosis. If you've ever driven somewhere and couldn't remember what happened on the drive, you've experienced it. And as we've already seen, altered states of consciousness seem commonplace when it comes to encountering the impossible.

The differences between the altered states we experience while driving, daydreaming, or at night are minimal, they each normally involve a low state of awareness regarding our surroundings as we focus our attention elsewhere, whether that be inwardly or on some other stimulus not involved with what we're doing at the time. Our bodies can continue to operate autonomously in this state, while our minds go somewhere else.

Furthermore, we might consider that reports of paranormal phenomena are often reported in liminal spaces because they happen to be more likely to induce the altered state of consciousness necessary to contact the things inhabiting this invisible world. Roadways are a nearly perfect combination of liminality and isolation, so it's no wonder they produce so many reports of the unexplained.

To be clear, I'm not suggesting that these phenomena are "all in our heads," so to speak, but rather, our heads are what ends up in these phenomena. Paranormal events seem to exist externally from our imaginations, it's just that they use the same mechanism through which we imagine in order to interact with us. A troubling component to this is that some instances of interaction seem to have physical effects, my friend's healed knee, for instance. What then, are we to make of that?

We may have to consider that consciousness is able to affect the material world. Quantum physicists have longed posited that observers affect that which they observe through the act of observation itself, perhaps even collapsing waveforms and fixing them into a static state. Could attention be the mechanism used by one of these beings to collapse waves of probability into a desired result, perhaps even, as we'll see in our next report, leaving a greasy smear on a windshield in accordance with the witness's expectations?

My friend Craig Nehring with Fox Valley Ghost Hunters contacted me via social media on Friday, April 13th, 2019, to alert me to a bizarre experience he'd had the night before at about 1 a.m. while driving near Wittenberg, Wisconsin.

So, last night while driving semi, [the weather] was sleet mixture [and it was] about 34 degrees [in temperature] …close to Wittenberg I got freaked out...it was dark outside. I was coming down one of the off ramps to stop for a soda. Something fell out of the sky that was really odd and I can't quite get the image out of my mind.

First off let me say it wasn't a bird or a bat, but this thing hit my window and mostly splattered on it. I saw it plain as day stuck to my window. I'd describe it as a small faerie if you believe in faeries, or possibly, I crap you not, a miniature mothman . It had small wings, [and] again, it wasn't a bat in the snow. It had long stretched out legs that came down below its body and had arms and fingers.

I was wide awake and not drowsy. I was going to take a picture, but it slid off the window leaving this massive gooey stain on my window which took several attempts with washer fluid to clean up off the window. I remember it was all black and I didn't see any eyes.

I was overwhelmed by the long legs and arms with small fingers. Those that know me and my team, know we don't post false info or tell tales on this site that are not true. I can tell you no trees were overhanging the highway and no bugs were out in this weather and the stain it left was so intense that it smeared the whole window. I also know what a flying squirrel looks like, and it was not that either. It's still imprinted in my eyes.

Size-wise [it was] eight inches high by five inches wide, with wings slightly wider.

I chatted with him online to get more details about his experience.

"The wings were the same color as the body. It seemed to have separation in the wings like maybe veins or arteries or bones," Nehring said.

"Considering the wings were kind of mashed on the windshield it was hard to tell [its wingspan], the body was about four inches with the wings going out further, say, about another four inches per side if they were not squashed."

Craig said he would have liked to get a photograph, but too many factors aligned to prevent it.

"I was in Shawano County on glare ice and rain in a semi, and not allowed to be on my phone," he said.

It was these same conditions that prevented him from stopping to look for a body.

"I was in an 80,000-pound semi," Craig explained. "I can't just stop and turn around in a sleet storm."

Interestingly, Craig's initial social media post elicited stories from others with similar experiences.

"I saw something at 15 and my friend who was with me saw it as well. We both can remember the moment clearly to this day...and it's been 34 years since that day," commented one person.

"I had a similar [sighting] only smaller in mid-afternoon near Wausau," commented another. "It left a real goo on the windshield. This was about 17 years ago and still etched in my memory. My son was like 12 years old at the time and riding with me. He did not see it, only the goo, and was perplexed that it was such an ugly shade of gray."

I've known Craig for years, and I don't believe he'd make up a story like this. Nor do I believe he hit something mundane like a bird or bat; neither one of those would have left the kind of gooey mess he described. Birds can leave behind a residue when striking a vehicle, but it's more likely to be a combination of powder down, a dry lubricant at the base of their feathers that crumbles a bit when birds preen, and some of the preening oil with which they dress their feathers. Bats, like most mammals, do secrete oil, but it's nothing like what Craig described.

I can't imagine an insect being responsible for the sighting, either, given the size description and time of year. Giant silk moths are found across North America, including Wisconsin, and while they can have a wingspan of up to seven inches, they don't emerge from their cocoons until the weather warms up, usually May at the earliest. The likelihood of one coming out early during a mid-April sleet storm in northern Wisconsin isn't good. Never mind that neither birds, bats, nor insects match Craig's description of what he saw.

This habit of flying directly in front of cars is something we'll see often enough. It's as though whatever it is wants our attention, even if that means running the risk of hitting the occasional windshield.

In January of 2020, I was contacted by Karri, a woman who said that, in the late summer of 2009, she and her then-partner were travelling from Kenora, Ontario, to Winnipeg, Manitoba, in Canada, when they saw a "large, human, bat-like being" fly across the road in front of them.

It has taken me many, many years to begin to research what I witnessed in the summer of 2009. I am 41 years old and tried to deny it, but I no longer can. I was not alone [during my sighting], I was with my partner of 11 years at the time. He and I are both artists and tattooed out of a Canadian town called Kenora, [but were] born in Winnipeg. We would drive back to Winnipeg weekly to visit family and friends, and [spend] a week in each place.

We were driving from Kenora to Winnipeg in the evening time, [along] a slit double-sided highway [called] Highway Number 1. It's a very common area for deer so your eyesight as passenger is [used] watching for deer, and that's when we both saw it. It was a matter of seconds, but we saw a black void in the lights of oncoming cars on the opposite side of the highway; [at first] thinking it was probably a deer, when our head lights [caught] it. I know what I saw and [my partner] saw the very same thing; it was a black-skinned, bald, [unclothed] human, but it was flying lower to ground-height of our Tacoma trucks lights, and it shielded its face from the light by flipping its wing up.

I've tattooed bat images before, and the webbing skin in a wing with the veining is thin—it was just like that. I could only describe it as a human bat, but [it had] no hair that I saw; [instead it had] more textured skin.

I know I sound crazy, but that is what we saw, and it's haunted me ever since. I tried to look into it straight after but was too scared. It made [me] question everything. I even went to see a priest...I've never spoken about this with strangers before, just close loved ones.

I hope this can help in your research and timeline. Thank you kindly, keep safe.

I corresponded with Karri via email to get further details of her sighting.

"It was the very end of our Canadian summer, in the end of July or beginning of August," Karri said. "We were traveling at a decent speed and [the creature] appeared to have a good speed of its own going. I'd like to say, by the time it had hit our side of the highway it was six feet [away from us] and its length would have me say it was over [six feet tall]."

"The time had been between 7 and 8 p.m., as we closed up shop at 6:30 p.m. and left from work to Winnipeg," she added. "Our sun sets at our closing time that time of year, and I know [the creature was close to our vehicle] because we slammed on the breaks. As far as wingspan, I could not tell you, but [the wings] appeared to be in proportion with its body. Wish I could tell you more details, but it was [over in a] matter of seconds. I just know that we saw black voids in front of other cars' headlights, and that when it was in front of ours, I saw what we both saw. A wing coming forward to shield its face and then it was gone."

Like others who have witnessed similar, seemingly impossible events, this experience left a lasting impression on Karri. However, unlike many other witnesses, she had the benefit of being believed by her parents and the family's priest.

"It made me feel shock and disbelief at first," she said. "It was honestly the scariest situation I had found myself in. We came into Winnipeg and both of us told our parents, convinced they would think us both to be crazy or on drugs, neither was the case, and both our parents believed us and said there are things in this world one cannot explain. [Our] priest gave us holy water and said 'We walk in the valley of death'; a saying I've heard growing up on occasion but didn't understand [until then]. I was terrified, the entire situation had me questioning everything I had known, [and] made me think of the world in an entirely different way."

"As pathetic as it sounds, we didn't go anywhere alone [after our sighting], even inside our cabin on the water, if I went pee or made a snack [my partner] came with me," she continued. "We didn't express what happened to [people other than our parents] at first, due to thinking people would say we've gone mad. I pondered if it was evil, if God rejected me. I really didn't know how to feel or think."

Over time, the profundity of the experience faded into the background.

"Once we moved back home, the feeling eventually eased up; much like a death you mourn for so long and with each day you slowly get back to life, not forgetting, just learning to live again," Karri explained. "It took me at least a year until I would go anywhere alone in the evening time. I've never in my life seen anything like this again."

Ultimately, Karri could find no easy answers to explain the encounter, although she has found some comfort in her faith.

"[I've] seen drawings that were similar, which made me feel less alone in it," she said. "I did get baptized years later, my partner never did. We were close friends for over 10 years before we got together and remained together for 11 years. This situation...we both don't have answers for what we saw, but we know in our souls what we felt and experienced to be true, and as a mature, aged adult now, I am still 100% sure as to what I saw in that brief moment, and no one could ever tell me otherwise."

Despite Karri's initial belief that no one would take her account seriously, similar sightings happen often enough that I've met dozens of other witnesses with experiences like her own.

In December of 2020, Jesse Durdel of the National Cryptid Society put me in contact with two young women who said that they had seen a large flying humanoid on Thanksgiving night.

The women's names have been changed to protect their identities.

Claire and Ashley, both of whom are 18-year-old women from Oregon, Wisconsin, told me in a phone interview that they'd seen an eight-to-nine-foot-tall creature with a wingspan of 10 to 15 feet while driving outside of town on November 26th.

Ashley said that she had initially seen something unusual while driving between Oregon and Stoughton on Highway 138 at around 10 p.m. that evening.

"I was on that road because I was going to Stoughton for some stuff," she said. "I was driving my car. I noticed this thing—I couldn't tell how big it was, it just looked like a black shadow—just start across the road, but it was probably a football field ahead of me. At first, I

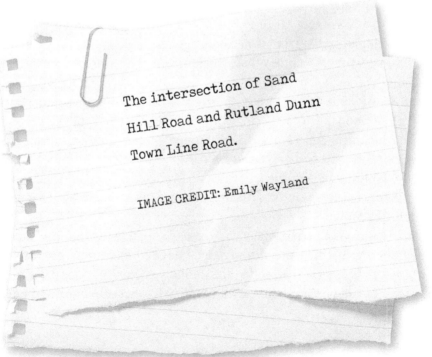

The intersection of Sand Hill Road and Rutland Dunn Town Line Road.

IMAGE CREDIT: Emily Wayland

thought it was my windshield, because I have cracks in my windshield, but that doesn't make sense because I've driven that road hundreds of times and I've never seen my windshield do anything like that. It was insanely fast. I was like 'I think I just saw something, but I'm not going to say anything because I'll sound crazy.'"

Later, at around 10:30 p.m., both women were going for a drive together when they said they saw a flying humanoid swoop across the road in front of them at the intersection of Sand Hill Road and Rutland Dunn Town Line Road.

"There was a possum in the road, and we stopped because we didn't want to hit it. We were driving around it, and then we looked up, and it was huge, like nine feet long," Claire said. "It was flying, and it swooped down across the road, and out of our sight. We were both like 'You saw that too, right?'"

"[The creature] was like a quarter of a football field ahead of us. It was really close. It was way too big to be a deer," Ashley continued. "It was kind of reddish brown in color, I want to say, but it was darker. If we hadn't stopped for that possum, it would have hit our car. That thing was huge. My first thought was 'Dear Lord, it's a pterodactyl.'"

A lamppost positioned at the intersection partially illuminated the being from underneath, they said, allowing them to determine its approximate color and dimensions.

According to the two women, the creature was headed north.

"It was too high up to be illuminated by the car's headlights. The very bottom was illuminated, but we couldn't see the top of it. It wasn't fully illuminated, but light was cast on the underside," Claire said. "Since it was at the intersection that we normally turned at—we normally turn at that intersection because we make loops around town—it swooped from the south towards the north. When you get to the intersection you have to turn north, and I was terrified to turn north. I didn't want to turn north."

Claire described the creature as looking "like Mothman," and said, "It looked like a very bulky person. Its limbs were a lot thicker than a human's [limbs] would be—a lot bigger around. It had these absolutely huge wings. There were arms on its side; actually, I didn't know if they were arms, there were appendages on its sides, and the wings were on its shoulders or back, but I couldn't really tell. I didn't see its head when it swooped down in front of us. I didn't see any head or neck when it swooped down."

They decided to continue their drive, eventually working up the courage to revisit the location of their sighting. At around 11 p.m., as they drove by the area again, Claire spotted something unusual in a nearby field.

Although the creature had first been seen heading north, when they returned, "it was standing on the south side [in a plowed down corn field]."

"We were at that point where we thought it would be gone, but then it wasn't," said Ashley.

Ashley, who was driving, didn't see the creature standing in the field. Claire, however, said she saw a strange creature with "very pronounced red eyes."

I looked out the back window and [the creature] was standing in the field. It was almost a full moon, so it was pretty illuminated. Its head didn't look like it had a neck, it looked like it was just an extension of its body. It looked like a human had tucked their head into their shoulders.

It had very pronounced red eyes. We didn't have any headlights in the back, and the only thing that would have reflected would have been the lamppost, so they were either reflecting really brightly or literally glowing. We go by that field all the time and I've never seen anything like that before or since.

The women described the creature as "super-fast," especially for its size.

"It was very fast, and the wings were very, very large," Claire said. "The body was so stocky. The silhouette was similar to how I would describe bigfoot, which I know, I'm using other known cryptids to describe this one, but that's really what it looked like. There was no pronounced neck, but it looked very stocky. It had very large, birdlike wings. I couldn't tell if it had feathers."

Ashley said that she thought that "the part illuminated by my headlights looked like reddish brown fur."

"It was either very fine feathers or fur," Claire agreed. "I didn't really see a texture. There weren't large feathers on the body—that I would have been able to see. The only thing I can say, is that when I saw the silhouette of it in the field, I could see jutting off points from the wings that I would call feathers, but I don't really know. It could just have wings shaped like that."

Both women said that they screamed after seeing the creature fly over the road, and Claire added that she "froze with fear" in response to the sighting.

"[I felt] fear, yeah, there was also the element of 'that's not supposed to be here,'" Ashley said. "You just know that whatever that is, it's not from around here. It's not supposed to be here."

"Yeah, like wrongness," added Claire. "We passed that place a couple more times, and the rest of the night we just got a weird there's-something-that-shouldn't-be-here feeling every time we were in that area."

They both also noticed other unusual phenomena happening that same evening, such as deer moving away from the spot where they had seen the creature and unusual interference on the car's radio.

"This was the weirdest thing that I noticed, it was way earlier, but it counts for the whole night basically. We kept seeing deer crossing the road," Ashley said. "I almost ran into two different deer on two different sides of town. Usually, if I see a deer at all, it's one deer a night. Oregon does not get a lot of deer, and I saw over seven deer that night. And we saw a whole herd running away from that spot."

"They were freaked out; they were running away. They were panicky," added Claire.

The radio, said Claire, "kept glitching like crazy, and it hasn't really done that before. It was cutting in and out, getting staticky, and then picking up another channel that was some gospel program. I know what channel that is and it's very far away from the channel we were on."

She added that the radio would glitch "only when we drove by that spot."

Only a few days later, on the evening of November 29th, Claire said she had another unusual sighting in "literally the same place."

"I saw a shadow on the road, because we drive the same route every time we drive," she said. "I saw a shadow that looked like it, and then something run into the trees, but it was...all I could really tell was that it was winged and very, very big, but I couldn't give you a definite shape."

Similar to the sighting reported by Claire and Ashley, a man in Woodstock, Illinois, reported a sighting of an eight-to-nine-foot-tall being "covered in dark fur" with large wings striding across the road on February 22nd, 2019. That witness said he thought the creature "may have been a bigfoot initially, but then noticed that it had a large set of membrane wings attached to the back, extending over the top of its head."

It was Lon who first received an email from the wife of a man who said her husband had encountered a strange being on the evening of February 22nd, 2019.

> My husband was returning home last night (February 22nd—approximately 8 p.m.) from a trip to Walgreens. While driving home, he saw something…coming across the road from the DuField Pond entrance on Country Club Road in Woodstock, Illinois. He said it was approximately one third the width of the road, eight to nine feet tall, and part of it looked leathery—but he wouldn't call it leather exactly.
>
> He is interested in speaking to you about it, but this afternoon he didn't seem ready to talk to you. I've asked him if he could sketch what he saw before he forgets. He indicated he's NOT going to forget this.
>
> Just wanted to give you a heads up and wondered if you have received any other reports in the Woodstock, IL vicinity.

That email was followed shortly by another that included a photograph of a footprint.

I was home when this happened, so didn't see anything. All I know is I believe my husband," she wrote. "I did go out to DuField this morning because we've had snow/ice/slush to see if I could see any traces of whatever this was. There were a lot of tracks/prints near the entrance—mostly boot prints, but some did not look like boots. However. It was hard to tell. I took photos/videos of the area."

Lon was the first to speak to the man over the phone.

"I talked to [the witness], who stated that he was driving on Country Club Road near the entrance to the Dufield Pond Conservation Area in Woodstock, Illinois. Suddenly, a large biped ran out onto the

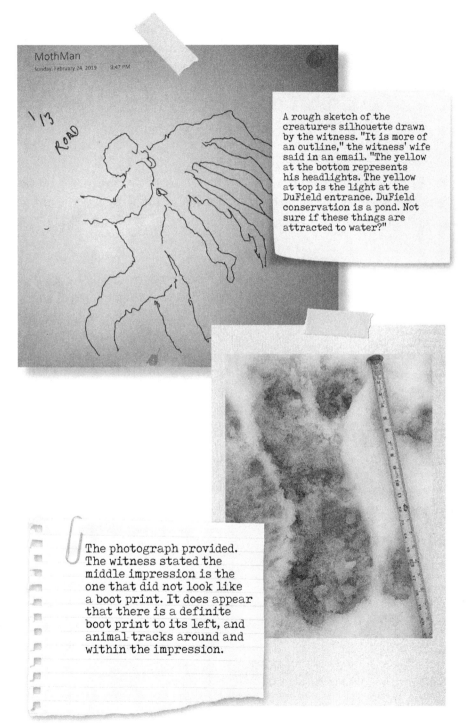

MothMan

Sunday, February 24, 2019   9:47 PM

1/13 ROAD

A rough sketch of the creature's silhouette drawn by the witness. "It is more of an outline," the witness' wife said in an email. "The yellow at the bottom represents his headlights. The yellow at top is the light at the DuField entrance. DuField conservation is a pond. Not sure if these things are attracted to water?"

The photograph provided. The witness stated the middle impression is the one that did not look like a boot print. It does appear that there is a definite boot print to its left, and animal tracks around and within the impression.

road approximately 30 feet ahead of him and quickly crossed to the opposite side," said Lon.

"He said that he thought that it may have been a bigfoot initially, but then noticed that it had a large set of membrane wings attached to the back, extending over the top of its head," he continued. "He described the shape of the wings as that of a gargoyle. The body was eight to nine feet in height and covered in dark fur. The arms and legs were well defined. He didn't notice any facial features. [He] got an excellent look at the creature since his headlights illuminated it and the light from the conservation area backlit it as well."

"He also stated that he had felt like it was a warning or harbinger of some kind," Lon added. "He did mention 'Nephilim' when discussing the encounter. [He said] it had upset him and that he was unable to talk about it until the next day."

I spoke to the man on February 25th, very soon after Lon had.

He was very forthright, and confirmed the testimony he'd given Lon, adding that there was a lone house across the street from Dufield Pond, but behind that was the McHenry County Fairgrounds. He said that he or his wife would visit the area to try and find better footprints in the mud but agreed that it might be best if Emily and I came down to investigate the area ourselves.

Emily and I visited the sighting area on March 9th and spoke to the witness and his wife. He reaffirmed his earlier testimony, emphasizing that he did not wish to embellish his story and would only recount the facts as he experienced them. Both the man and his wife are respected members of their community, and I appreciated them being willing to speak with us. Believe me when I say they had plenty to lose if a story like this got out and they were associated with it.

The couple very graciously took us to the area of the sighting, where we made a strange discovery. Among the other prints in the ice and snow—largely left by canines, ambulatory birds, and human boots—was an enormous humanoid print with what appeared to be individual toes. There was only one of them, but it was headed in the direction of Country Club Road. We didn't see anything else out of the ordinary and left soon after.

Just 15 miles northeast of Woodstock lies the village of Richmond, Illinois, where in October of 2019 a woman saw something very

The view facing the street from the driveway leading into Dufield Pond. This area is closed to regular vehicle traffic during the winter months.

PHOTO CREDIT: Emily Wayland

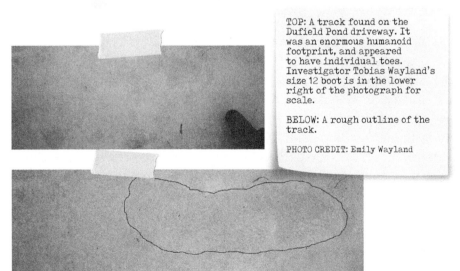

TOP: A track found on the Dufield Pond driveway. It was an enormous humanoid footprint, and appeared to have individual toes. Investigator Tobias Wayland's size 12 boot is in the lower right of the photograph for scale.

BELOW: A rough outline of the track.

PHOTO CREDIT: Emily Wayland

similar to the red-eyed being described by Claire.

Lon received the initial report of her sighting through an email.

Friday, October 5th, 2019, around 10 p.m. my [17-year-old] son and I were coming home through Richmond, Illinois. He wanted McDonald's. We took the back roads home (we live in Wisconsin on [the] border) and on Rt 173 and Broadway (I believe it's Broadway) we both saw something very tall (six to seven feet) hunched over looking with the brightest red eyes we've ever seen! It looked as if it were floating or hopping. We couldn't make out much as it was very dark, but it was not like any animal we've seen before! When I got home, I started Googling animals and found some Mothman myth.

I'm not sure what we saw but it was out of the ordinary. We take this road often but only a few times at night and had never seen this before. It was maybe 10 to 20 feet from our car and my son was freaking out telling me to go, so we didn't stop. Our family thinks we're crazy and teases us [that] we saw a zombie, so I'd prefer this to stay anonymous. I came across your info and thought I'd share. We didn't notice any wings, but it was dark out. We both thought it was hopping like a kangaroo, and now I'm curious if there are any other odd sightings in this area.

Lon was later able to talk to the witness by telephone.

"She had left work late on Friday, October 5th, 2019, and had picked up her 17-year-old son on the way home. The time was approximately 10 p.m. They [were] on Route 173 (Kenosha Street) and Broadway Road, on their way to a McDonald's. They were also adjacent to the North Branch Conservation Area," he said. "They both noticed a pair of very bright red eyes along the side of the road. The creature was about seven feet in height and dark in color. It was stooped or hunched over, as if something heavy was attached to its back. The witnesses never saw wings, but it seemed some structure was on its back. As they approached it, the creature looked at them and started to 'hop' back. They had gotten very close to it, about 20 feet or less. As it hopped back towards the field, they looked back, and it seemed that it suddenly disappeared. It never took flight. [The witness] stated that the eyes were similar to two very bright lights [that] emanated from within the creature. [She] wanted to turn around and look again, but her son was totally freaked out by the encounter and insisted she continue driving."

"The witness had no indication of the winged humanoid sightings in and around Chicago," he added. "She immediately began to research her sighting and found my information."

Not long after that, I spoke with the witness myself.

She described to me how she was struck by the creature's eyes.

"The first thing I saw were these red, glowing eyes. They were really bright, it was different. It wasn't glowing like a normal animal, like eyeshine. They looked like they were producing their own glow. That's what was super weird about it," she said.

The woman began to slow down as she realized she was seeing something very strange.

I slowed down a lot, and it looked really tall, I'd say six or seven feet. It was hunched over, and it looked like it was either hopping or floating going towards the field—there's a big, open field there. It looked like it was looking at us. I didn't say anything to my son. Then I started slowing down more, and he started flipping out.

He said "What are you doing? Go! What the hell is that?"

I said "Okay, so you saw it, too."

I'd never even heard the word before, but he said "It's some type of cryptid! You're taking a back road, are you nuts? Get the hell out of here!"

Then it was just kind of gone. I don't know if it turned around, if it had closed its eyes or what. We didn't see anything fly up.

But he saw the same thing I did, because he said "It was huge. It was super tall, it had the weirdest eyes, and it was hopping or floating."

He saw the same thing as me.

It was cloudy that night, and it was difficult for the woman to see much beyond the thing's eyes because it was outside the range of her car's headlights, but she was able to make out some details.

"It was really hard to see, because it was dark, but its upper body looked bulky and hunched over," she said. "I wouldn't be able to tell you if it had anything [like wings] attached to its back or not. It just definitely looked hunched over, and then the way it was moving, no animals around here float or hop."

Normally, said the woman, she would have stopped and tried to take a picture.

"I didn't feel scared. I was just like, 'What the heck was that?'" she said. "I wanted to go back, but [my son] was freaking out. He didn't want to turn around. He said, 'Just get home.'"

As for what she saw that night, she isn't exactly sure, she only knows it was far outside of her normal experience.

"It was definitely different. The eyes were definitely something I'd never seen before," she said. "I just couldn't comprehend what it was and what I was seeing."

Emily and I visited the sighting area later that month and took some photographs. We didn't see any red-eyed monsters, but everything else was where the woman said it was and we were able to confirm that she would have had a clear view of anything standing in the spot she saw the creature.

Just over a year later, we found ourselves in Oregon, Wisconsin, chasing similar high strangeness.

We went to the site of Claire and Ashley's encounter twice, the first time at approximately 10:30 p.m. on December 11th and again at around 2 p.m. about a week later. It's a lonely intersection in rural Wisconsin, decorated by a single tall streetlight. A few houses dot the street at irregular intervals, the spaces between them filled with trees and farmers' fields. Traffic is light and the road feels isolated, especially at night.

Emily and I brought our recording equipment, a handful of cameras that we use to shoot video, and although I would normally insist that we turn off the car's radio while filming at a sighting location, given what Claire and Ashley reported, I thought this time maybe we'd leave it on.

We didn't notice any obvious radio interference either time, however, upon review of the footage we recorded during our initial visit, we did notice some very unusual audio interference on both cameras used during the investigation. The same interference was present upon review of the footage taken on our second trip, although it was much lighter.

Strangely, the interference was only recorded in the immediate area of the sighting. We could mark the phenomenon's boundaries by watching the video; one second there's no interference, the next it's there, and then when we've travelled outside of its influence, it disappears, but when we turn around to head back the way we'd come, there it is again in the exact same spot. The oddest thing about it, the thing that I just couldn't ignore, was that the sphere of influence for this audio interference was centered on the intersection where Claire and Ashley had seen the winged creature swoop in front of them. The exact spot where they'd said their radio repeatedly glitched the night of their sighting.

We drove up and down that street, looking for anything that could have caused it; ham radio antennas, electrical transformers, satellite dishes, anything at all, but ultimately, we came up empty. That the mysterious interference was much quieter the second time we visited the sighting location made me wonder if its source hadn't been weakened somehow. It was as if a window had opened the night of the young women's sighting and had been slowly closing ever since.

Whatever these windows are and wherever they lead, one seemed to have also opened in Cape Girardeau, Missouri, for a span of several weeks in the late summer and early fall of 2020.

I received the reports out of order, the chronologically later report leading to the earlier one in a way common to paranormal investigation. Witnesses often doubt that anyone has ever before seen, or would believe, what they've experienced, and they're reluctant to come forward as a result. Only after seeing someone else report something similar do these witnesses gather the courage to share their own experience. I often wonder how many stories are still out there, hidden among the population in areas where nobody has yet been the first to come forward.

In October of 2020, I received a message from a woman who wished to report her sighting of a "black, humanoid figure with very large wings and legs" in Cape Girardeau, Missouri.

According to the woman, the sighting took place while heading east on Bertling Street, near the Southeast Missouri State Softball Field, between 8 and 9 p.m. on October 8th.

I was able to interview this witness over the phone, although she did insist that I keep her identity a secret. That goes for any witness in these pages who's chosen anonymity; I know and have confirmed their identity, but I won't betray their trust by sharing it without permission.

"Me, my two girls, and my fiancé went to a little street area where the houses have Halloween decorations at nighttime," she told me. "We went down one way and then came back the other way to look at both sides of the street. We did that, and we were headed back home. We came up over a hill and when we got down almost to the stop sign, that's when I saw it. It was like a human figure, but with big wings—the feet and toes were pointed to the ground—it had scrawny legs but muscled at the calf. The feet were long but pointy. It was maybe six feet tall. The wings weren't open, they were still closed."

The creature's wings, which she said looked like they were made of skin, "were really pointy and they were past its head. [The creature] just looked like somebody getting ready to dive off of something, like they have their hands out. The wings were over top of it, and they were pulled in, like wrapped around it. The wings weren't as long as the body. They came out over the head but were shorter than the legs."

Its head, she added, was "really little and round—kind of pointed but round."

The creature, which she estimated to have been around 100 feet from the car, looked like it had just "leaped from the trees" to the right of the road.

"About 100 feet from the stop sign to the right is a grove of tall trees," the woman said. "About two to three acres of big, tall trees. That's where I saw it. [The creature] looked like it had leaped or dove. It was higher than the streetlights, but not real high—midway over the road, but in the sky."

Although the being was black, she was still able to see it because "the light from the softball field lit it some." The dark figure stood out against the sky, as it was "blacker than the night itself."

She said it didn't look like the creature had any fur or feathers.

"It was bigger than a bird, it didn't look like a bird," she explained. "When I saw it, it was kind of like [the monster from] Jeepers Creepers."

The woman asked her fiancé if he'd seen it, too, and he thought he had caught "maybe a little bit of it."

She estimated that the sighting lasted only six to eight seconds.

After her sighting, the woman looked online to see if anyone else had seen something similar, and found an article published by The Singular Fortean Society about a man who said that he and his son encountered a strange flying creature near West Alton, Missouri, in 2016. That sighting was originally reported to Lon over at Phantoms & Monsters.

Lon had originally received an email in 2018 from a man who said that he and his son had seen "a huge black thing...like a well-built man with long legs" and "very wide" wings while duck hunting.

In mid-November 2016, my son and I had been duck hunting from a blind in the Upper Mississippi Waterfowl Area, not far from West Alton, Missouri. It was about 5:15 p.m. and we were walking back to my truck. I had parked in a small lot off of Harbor Point Rd. and we had to walk about 500 yards.

As we walked along the road, my son noticed a huge black thing descending towards the water's edge. I had never seen anything that large flying anywhere. It definitely wasn't a bald eagle or a crane, and as it got closer to the ground, we were both shocked that it looked like a human!

It wasn't flapping its wings but was gliding on a slow downward angle. It was about 50 yards from us, but there was enough light that we could clearly see it. The wings were outstretched and were very wide. The wing shape was similar to that of a bat, but huge! The color was dark, almost black. The body was tapered like a well-built man with long legs. The head was small compared to the body, so I definitely knew it was not human. We were both caught off-guard and were mesmerized by what we were seeing. It landed in the thick weeds by the water and was obscured from our sight.

At that point, we both wanted to get out of there because we had no idea what this thing was. As we quickly walked along the road, we saw this thing crawling out of the weeds and into a small clearing. It was literally pushing itself forward on the ground with its legs and wings in the direction of the water. We could hear the sound it was making as it "crawled" on the damp ground and mud. It didn't look like it was struggling, but it was an awkward way to move around. Though it had legs, I could not make out what we would think were feet. I assumed this was the way it actually moved on the ground. It slid into the water, then raised up a few times; like a swimmer doing a breast stroke. Then it disappeared into the murky water.

My son will not go to that location anymore, but I'd really like to know what we saw. I told a co-worker, who is also a duck hunter, about the incident. He seemed interested at the time, but I'm sure he doesn't believe me. I've never heard of anything similar to this thing, either around here or anywhere else. Do you have any idea of what this was? I saw your Google ad for humanoid sightings, so I looked you up. We can talk if you'd like. Thanks.

Lon was able to speak to the witness by telephone the following day.

"I asked the witness why he waited so long to contact anyone," Lon said. "He said that it took him a while to actually believe what he and his son had seen was real."

The witness described the creature's wingspan as approximately 12-15', and the structure of the wings as very wide and bat-like.

"[The witness] also said that the head was small and kind of shaped like a football with a slight point on the top. He did not see detached arms, but by the way it moved along the ground, the arms were most likely part of the wings," said Lon

The creature reportedly made no sounds other than those caused by its crawling.

"I also asked if they had a cell phone with them and why they hadn't taken photos," he added. "[The witness] said he didn't even realize that until they got back to the car."

The witness's son has so far refused to discuss the incident.

West Alton is approximately 125 miles north of the sighting area in Cape Girardeau.

Our witness of the "black, humanoid figure with very large wings and legs" in Cape Girardeau was similarly unable to take any photos.

"I was going to get my phone out [to record it], but then I thought 'What if it sees me and tries to come after me?' I'd never seen or read about anything like that until I looked it up to see if anybody else had seen any other bat-looking humans. It was a shock to see something like that. It is a little scary to go out at night and know something like that's out there," she told me.

That fear of reprisal, of not quite knowing what the consequences of interference might be but knowing that they'll be bad, we see that a lot, especially when it comes to flying humanoids. I noticed it when I first started covering these cases, and then compiling the information for my last book, *The Lake Michigan Mothman: High Strangeness in the Midwest,* really drove the point home. There's an element of fear present, not just in the 'Mothman' cases, but in almost all of them that we investigate; sometimes it's lurking just below the surface, disguised as a sort of commonsense tinged with awe, and sometimes it's radiating from witnesses in waves of panic, but it's still there, all the same. Something about all of this is very threatening when it wants to be.

A few weeks after the sighting of a "black, humanoid figure with very large wings and legs," I spoke with two sisters who said that in August of 2020 they'd seen a strange, flying creature in almost the same spot.

The two women were driving at about 6 o'clock in the evening on Lexington Avenue and had just passed Sprigg Street when they had their encounter, which took place only about a mile from the previously reported sighting.

Beverly Weakley, 67, was behind the wheel while Brenda Elfrink, 60, was in the passenger seat.

Brenda was looking at her phone when she heard her sister exclaim, "What was that?"

"I was on my phone, I heard her, and I looked up. I got a good look at it, but I didn't really know what I was looking at. It seemed like it was just across the road and gone. There was no place for it to land," said Brenda.

She described the creature as being "big and blackish/brownish—more brown than black, but dark" and "shaped like nothing I've ever seen. I saw a lot of movement like wings—I saw more of that than anything else."

"I'd say it was five or six feet tall, maybe bigger. I was kind of rationalizing what I was looking at. There were no feet, I just saw a big brown mass, basically. But it did feel like I saw movement, like wings

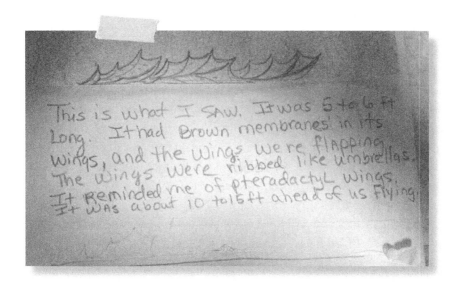

This is what I saw. It was 5 to 6 ft Long. It had brown membranes in its wings, and the wings were flapping. The wings were ribbed like umbrellas. It reminded me of pteradactyl wings. It was about 10 to 15 ft ahead of us flying.

A sketch made by Beverly Weakley describing what she saw.

or something," Brenda said. "I saw a whipping, fluttering motion and it looked like it almost took up the whole road. It probably didn't, but that's what it looked like to me. I honestly wondered at first if it was a big throw rug flying across the road and whipping up in the wind or something, but there was no wind. It wasn't a stormy day or anything. I said, 'Oh my god, we saw Mothman.'"

However, said Brenda, her sister Beverly "saw much more" of the thing than she did.

According to Beverly,

It looked like it might have come from the side of the road, there are some trees there, but it was fully in our vision in the car. It wasn't high, it was maybe eight feet off of the ground—you could see underneath it, you could see over it. It was probably five to six feet long, and it was brown. It didn't look like it had feathers to me, it looked like it had membranes. It looked like it had webbed, membranous wings, and there were a lot of wings. Some were flapping. They were ribbed like umbrellas. It didn't look like a pterodactyl, but it looked like that kind of wings. It was probably 10 to 15 feet ahead of us, and it was flying. I didn't see a person, like a body shape, but it certainly could have been a thin something that was long.

Beverly said the creature "looked like something was shrouded in this bunch of wings. It got skinnier towards the last two feet, like they were wrapped around. To me, it looked like a body shrouded in wings. It was definitely wings of some sort, and they looked like they were meat, not feathers. I didn't see any limbs; I didn't see a head."

The 67-year-old described the wings moving in an undulating fashion, "like a wave."

"The wings were moving," she explained. "It looked like it had taken off and it had these little wings throughout. The way it flew was weird. It didn't use all of its wings at one time. It was the strangest thing I've ever seen. It rippled, kind of."

Neither woman was able to tell where the creature went after it flew across the road.

"I was driving, so I didn't see where it went," Beverly said. "I don't know why we didn't try to stop and look some more, but it was scary. I think that's why."

As for Brenda, she "didn't see as much" as Beverly, because she "just looked up and glanced."

"I didn't see all that detail," she said. "I did see a glimpse of a fluttering wing or something, but not all the detail [Beverly] saw."

Although the sighting lasted only several seconds, both women stuck by their story despite the skepticism expressed by those close to them and emphasized that they did not wish to embellish their testimony in any way. In fact, if it wasn't for Brenda's son mentioning the report from October, they may never have reported their own sighting.

Brenda said that, following their sighting, "Everybody was saying 'Oh, you saw an owl,' or whatever. I just shut up, because everybody was acting like I'm crazy."

"We went home kind of scared, and [Beverly's] family acted like we were crazy. I honestly don't know how I could shut up about it, because I know what I saw. I just kind of let it go, until [my son] said that people started seeing it," she explained. "What makes this so funny or odd, is that [my son] messaged me and asked if I'd heard of all these sightings. Before I heard anything that he'd had to say, I told him what we saw. I told him where we'd seen it, and he said 'Mom, that's the same area.' If we'd have turned instead of going straight, we would have ended up where the [October sighting happened]."

Beverly added, "My husband said it was a pile of leaves that were swirling. No, it's not. That's not what it was. A crane? No, it wasn't a crane. I know a crane. It was very unusual and unsettling. That's why we started talking about it again. We saw something in the same area [as the other sighting], and I cannot tell you what it was."

"I'm so glad you called," she confided in me. "Because I wanted to tell somebody, but we just didn't know what to do with the information, so we just didn't do anything. Then we heard talk again, and it's the same area."

Beverly's description of what she saw reminded me of the seraphim referred to in the Bible. Not in the sense that I believe the phenomena experienced by people today are angels as defined by the Abrahamic religions, but in the sense that they might share a common origin; one as mysterious today as it was when our ancestors encountered it thousands of years ago. The narratives have changed, but the story remains the same.

According to the Book of Isaiah 6:2, "Above him were seraphim, each with six wings: With two wings they covered their faces, with two they covered their feet, and with two they were flying."

The Book of Isaiah is one of the Books of the Prophets, describing the prophecies of Isaiah as he is called to be God's messenger to the people of Israel. It's a book of illumination and inspiration. I'm left wondering if these experiences would have made more sense to our ancestors; if we're too disconnected from our spiritual, intuitive selves to properly interpret them. Some say that glossolalia is the language of angels, well, what if the structure of that language is formed of symbols and revelatory experiences? That's not a language in which many people will still be fluent in the modern age.

Maybe that's the problem. We've lost touch with who we were and these otherworldly intelligences struggle to keep up with who we are. Like completely foreign ships in the night, we each shine our beacons in a code only we understand, desperately trying to communicate in a language whose mannerisms are similar but whose meanings are indecipherable.

Perhaps it's time we stopped obsessing over merely finding the messages and started concentrating on learning the language.

CHAPTER 7

THE STRANGEST DOG YOU'VE EVER SEEN

These experiences have a way of twisting our perception, often making us doubt our senses. It may be that this is an intentional obfuscation by the entities, or perhaps they're merely reacting to our own indecision regarding what we expect to see. Either option is equally disconcerting to those who encounter the impossible.

In January of 2019, my and Emily's friend Adam Benedict of the Pine Barrens Institute brought to our attention a report he'd received from a woman who said she and her husband had seen a bizarre, chimeric creature in the spring of 2013 near Beloit, Wisconsin. The area in which the sighting took place is on the edge of town, where a few houses give way to rows of corn fields.

In her initial email to Adam, the witness said that she and her husband had "just turned off Burton Street onto McKinley Avenue" and were "driving towards Newark Road" at approximately 4 p.m., when "across the field on the right we saw an animal by the tree line."

Her husband, who was driving, slowed down to get a better look at it, but traffic behind them forced the couple to keep driving. During their initial pass they saw an animal that "seemed to be on its back legs by a tree."

"It was barrel-shaped, and we were wondering if it was a bear. It dropped to all fours and started moving," the witness wrote. "We were debating if it was a bear, wild boar or the strangest dog we have ever seen."

Despite the woman's reservations that the animal would be gone if they went back, her husband decided to turn the car around for a second look. They drove back down McKinley, and performed a U-turn on Burton Street, which once again put the animal to their right. The pair pulled their car over onto the shoulder, and that's when, according to the woman, "everything just gets weird."

In a second email to Adam, she went into greater detail regarding the sighting.

Up until this point I objectively believe my husband and I and the people in the car behind us saw a strange animal in the field. The rest of this story is my subjective experience.

The animal was coming towards us. It moved like a cat, graceful with a long, flicky tail. It didn't look like a cat though, except for the head. It was dark, but not black, brindled, dark browns with some black. The fur was short like a dog with some glossiness to it.

Its head was massive and triangle-shaped, the eyes were large and green. The head looked so robust, like you could hit it with a bat, and it would break the bat. It was flat like a cat, no snout like a dog or bear. Its chest was also triangle-shaped and really muscular with legs that came down like a bulldog. The back end was a smaller triangle with legs that came off like a German Shepard. This thing was big and solid muscle. I think the top of its head would of came to my chin, so about four feet.

The tail was about the same length as the body.

The animal then began to amble towards them from about halfway across the field.

"This was what was confusing, it moved like a cat, but didn't look like one," she explained. "The whole time I had the feeling it knew we were watching and found the situation amusing. Also, the longer you watched it the harder it became to see it. Like its edges were blurring. It got to about 30 feet from the road and lied down, in a 'C' shape, just like a cat. It was staring at us, and I was staring at it. But the longer I looked at it, it almost seemed to become pixelated."

The couple then reportedly felt a sudden, overwhelming fear; something that has had a profound effect on how they chose to interpret the experience as individuals.

"I don't know how long this lasted, with a feeling of amusement on its side and wonder and confusion on our part," the witness said. "It changed in a heartbeat, the feeling that it could come through my window and bite my head off and my husband hitting the gas both seemed to happen at the same time."

"I looked at him and he goes 'how was there no traffic?' It seemed like we had been parked for at least five minutes," she continued. "Then he said it was a dog. It was said in the tone of voice that says 'please let that of been a dog.' If you ask him now, he will tell you we saw a deformed dog. I think he really needs it to be a dog, where I'm okay with living with not ever knowing. We were at the stop sign on Newark Road when it hit me that I was an idiot because I had my phone and could have taken a picture."

I was able to contact the woman and speak to her over the phone. She confirmed the details of her report to Adam with no embellishment and was consistent throughout the conversation.

"The more we tried to look at it the more confused we got," she explained. "It was laughing at us…it knew we were confused."

Towards the end of the encounter, the creature was only 20 to 30 feet from their vehicle, but they still were having trouble focusing on the details of its appearance.

"The edges of it were getting fuzzy. You couldn't focus on it," said the witness. "The harder you tried to look at it the less you were actually seeing."

And what their minds were able to comprehend simply did not seem right.

"Everything about it was wrong," she said. "It was just like nothing fit."

The woman also told me that the next day a friend and coworker confessed that she had experienced a similar event in the area.

"She's a hunter and she had no idea what she was looking at," she said of her friend's encounter. "That's the part that kind of bothers me the most."

When asked if the creature might have been a ranging mountain lion, the woman was certain that it was not.

"I know what that kind of cat looks like," she said. "This thing was massive…a solid 300 lbs. Its head was triangular, and its eyes were far to the sides."

"I grew up in the country," she added. "I've lived in this area my entire flipping life. The emotion was different [in this sighting]. We've seen stuff we couldn't immediately identify, but it didn't have this kind of 'through the looking glass' feeling."

Emily and I traced the path taken by this woman and her husband on that day, and while we didn't encounter any phantom chimeras, everything else was right where she said it was.

Several months after I spoke with this woman, we were contacted at The Singular Fortean Society by a man who said that he and his wife were driving home when they encountered a bizarre creature crossing the road just outside of Rockton, Illinois.

Rockton is only about five miles south of Beloit, and the man contacted us after seeing the previous report. Emily and I made the trip down to scout this area, too, and like the other site, it's in that liminal space where civilization slowly gives way to nature.

According to his testimony,

My wife and I were driving home the evening of August 8th, 2019. It was a little past 11 p.m. We were on South Bluff Road, heading north, having just turned off of Prairie Hill Road near the bridge.

As we turned the corner, she first spotted "it" on the right side of the road, nearest the river. She spotted eyes reflecting light, and assumed it was a normal animal (opossum or raccoon). I saw movement and said "deer", as whatever it was had longer front legs, like a tall dog. Then, as it crossed the road in front of us, we realized it was not a deer. Or any other easily recognized animal.

I have grown up in rural areas and am well acquainted with various rural creatures. This was not a coyote or fox. It had a rounded head and a flat face, no snout or muzzle. It had no obvious ears, or they were very tight against its head. Dark brown in color, almost muddy red in the car headlights. Long, slim tail that curled under as it loped across the road. It moved in a way that could only be compared to an ape or bear's style of movement, as if all fours were faster but not completely necessary. My wife and I thought it moved like a gibbon. It left a bizarre impression on us both, as we can't settle on a creature that we believe it could be.

The chimeric creature he described was eerily like the one I'd heard about less than a year before.

He even reported a similar feeling of high strangeness during his encounter.

"There was definitely a sense of oddity, even now my head is trying to wriggle up a fit as to what it was. The whole incident lasted only a second or two," he said. "Amusingly, I live within five minutes of the first sighting."

He added that he has had some experience with the unknown before the sighting, but none since—although his encounter with the phantom chimera did happen very recently.

"I actually have been quite interested in the grand 'fortean unknown' for a long time. I've been part of a few 'haunt hunts,' present at a seance or two. I've been to Bachelor's Grove, Gettysburg, and the grave of Inez Clark. Since [this sighting]? Not really. Been fairly quiet," he said.

He also shared a news article he had found from early July of 2019 in which a mountain lion was reportedly seen near Beloit by Or-fordville resident Luke Reints. Interestingly, when interviewed by local news, Reints never described a mountain lion; he said only that he had seen an animal resting underneath a bridge along the Rock River.

"I saw something out of the corner of my eye," he said. "It was kind of moving a little bit. I got the chills right away. I just started back-ing up all the way to my truck."

By the time Reints returned to the scene with a police officer, the animal was gone.

Maybe by that time the message had been delivered, whatever it was, although he may not have been able to speak the language neces-sary to fully understand it.

CHAPTER 8
REMEMBER TO LOOK UP

Airports are an often-overlooked liminal space. On a physical level, they're massive campuses designed to transition us from one area to another, continually shuffling us toward our destination or holding us temporarily in stasis as we await our delivery. But beyond that, many airports can be confounding labyrinths to the uninitiated, inducing an almost otherworldly confusion with their constant traffic and overwhelming sensory displays. It's no wonder, then, that airports can often be at the center of impossible experiences.

Famously, in 2006, a dozen United Airlines employees, corroborated independently by other witnesses, reported a disc-shaped object hovering over O'Hare International Airport in Chicago, Illinois. The Federal Aviation Administration tried to explain it away as a "weather phenomenon," submitting that the pilots, ground crews, and other professionals had been fooled by a circular hole in the clouds. This explanation went over like a lead balloon, and the case remains one of ufology's best known unexplained cases to this day.

O'Hare has been of particular interest to Emily and me over the past few years. So far, at least a dozen sightings of flying humanoids and related phenomena have been reported out of the airport, although often with considerable variability in their credibility. One of the chief investigators of the phenomena in and around O'Hare is Manuel Navarette, someone with whom we've worked closely on the Lake Michigan Mothman investigation. But in March of 2020, Manuel ceased being only an investigator on the case and became a witness.

About three months prior to Manuel's sighting, I had spoken to a man who said that he'd seen a red-eyed, winged humanoid while driving near O'Hare on the night of December 6th, 2019.

The witness, who agreed to the use of his first name, Daniel, said that he works in cargo for an airline in the airport and had left work early that night to go meet friends.

"I was the last one to get out of work," he said. "I normally work until 11 pm, but we got out a little earlier than expected. Around 10:15 or 10:20 p.m. is when I left. I [was driving] down West Higgins, and I was headed to the bar to meet up with one of my friends from work. [To my left, in a large patch of grass] is where I saw it."

"It was dark, and there's a building with a certain amount of light [near the sighting area]. I was able to take a glimpse at it while I was driving," Daniel continued. "I saw headlights coming towards me as well. I'm always looking at that side because there's deer there. I'm always eager to look there to see them. I can tell the difference between a deer and what I saw. What I saw was not a deer."

According to Daniel, the creature he saw matched exactly what was described by a witness who said that, just over a week before Daniel's sighting, he had seen a seven-foot-tall "person with wings" near the loading dock for Nippon Cargo Airlines. Except, said Daniel, the thing he saw had red eyes. He said he was able to estimate the creature's height by comparing it to a nearby fence.

But the similarities didn't end with a physical description; present, too, was the feeling of evil described by the previous witness.

That first witness was a man who said he was standing outside of a cargo dock at O'Hare when he spotted a seven-foot-tall "person with wings" just outside of a fence by the parking lot. The sighting reportedly took place at approximately 6:30 p.m. on November 26th, 2019.

The sighting was investigated by Manuel, and according to the report he received from the man,

> I was at the airport picking up a load at Nippon [Cargo Airlines], I was already backed into a dock and was standing away from the truck smoking a cigarette while they loaded my truck. I was looking toward the runways, in the direction of the tunnel and that is when I noticed something that looked like a large bird standing just outside of the fence by the parking lot. It was not hard to miss because two streetlamps were nearby. It looked like a person with wings that were stretched out and flapping. It was walking away from the fence toward the open field and then began to flap its wings and disappeared.

Manuel was able to speak with the witness over the phone.

"I spoke with the witness via phone and was able to get a little more information regarding this sighting," the investigator said. "The witness primarily speaks Spanish but was able to report this sighting with the help of his daughter and her boyfriend."

"[He] was standing away from his truck as it was being loaded, smoking a cigarette, when he said he caught movement out of the corner of his eye and saw the being standing near the parking lot [that] was illuminated by two streetlamps. The witness stated that the creature was about seven feet tall using the fence as a point of reference," Manuel explained. "When I asked him how he was able to be so certain as to the height of this being, the driver stated he has been to this location multiple times and he estimates the fence to be about eight feet high. Using the fence, he was certain that the being was at least seven feet tall. When I asked him how large the wings were, he said at least six feet across and black."

The witness used language also seen in earlier sighting reports from the largely Hispanic neighborhood of Chicago's Little Village.

"When I asked him to describe the being he said it looked like a demonio (demon) or a duende (goblin) and was solid black. The witness said he saw nothing that looked like eyes and he assumed the creature might have had his back turned to him. He stated that it walked with a gait like a bird and that it was flapping its wings as it walked toward the large field that is by the runways, and disappeared into the night," Manuel said. "The witness did state that when it disappeared, he quickly did the sign of the cross and asked the Virgin Mary for protection. He put out his cigarette and quickly walked back to his truck. When I asked him why he did that, he stated that he felt a presence that was evil and was convinced that he had seen a demon. When asked to elaborate on this statement the witness refused to talk about it anymore for fear of it coming back."

That fear of reprisal for talking about their sighting is something I've seen out of witnesses myself more than once while investigating these Lake Michigan Mothman sightings.

"I respected his wishes and went on to ask other questions about the time, conditions and if there were other potential witnesses to his sighting," Manuel continued. "He stated that there were others at the same facility, but many were either inside the facility itself or in their trucks. When asked if he had seen something similar before, the witness stated that he had when he was a teenager back home in Mexico. The witness stated that he saw a solid black, winged creature that was circling an open field that he and other children were playing soccer in. He stated it circled the field and made a loud screeching noise before flying off into the surrounding forest. When I asked him if he remembered the date of the sighting, he stated that he did not remember the exact date, but a week later there was a large earthquake in Mexico City. For the record, the magnitude 8.0 earthquake that hit Mexico City was on September 19, 1985."

"The witness seemed sincere, albeit scared that he had seen something demonic and evil. It is my opinion that the witness is telling the truth. An investigator will be dispatched to do a field observation and any info will be posted on [UFO Clearinghouse] as it becomes available," he added.

Daniel said that he was ready to dismiss his sighting until he found an article online describing the other man's experience.

"That was really weird because, honestly, I thought I was going crazy at first. I said to myself, 'No, that can't be it. I don't think I saw that,'" he said. "After that, once I saw the article [the day after my sighting], I thought 'Okay, I must not be going crazy, because Nippon is not far from where [my sighting took place].' That was the craziest part. I kind of freaked out. I saw that something wasn't right. I saw it the same way that the other gentleman saw it. It felt really evil. It had those red eyes. How could any creature have those?"

"I thought I was going crazy, man. I thought I was going crazy, until I read the article. I must not be the only one who's seeing this stuff," Daniel added. "Maybe it was just the fear I felt, but honestly, it didn't feel good at all. It was one of the creepiest things I've ever seen in my life."

Lon also spoke to this witness, and later told me that he found his testimony to be credible. When we compared notes, it was apparent that Daniel had not deviated from his story when relating it to either of us.

A few months later, I became aware of the sighting had by Manuel after he posted a request for someone to call him in a Phantoms & Monsters Fortean Research Team shared message thread on the morning of March 3rd. I called him shortly thereafter.

I could hear the excitement in Manuel's voice as he related his experience to me; it was clear something had happened.

"I was driving to work, taking my usual route on Mannheim Road, and I'm talking to my wife on the phone," he said. "So, I'm talking, and I'm coming up to the [intersection of Mannheim Road and Zemke

Boulevard]—on the right side of it is an old Enterprise Rent-A-Car lot that used to be there, but they moved it to the other side of the airport. The building is still there and everything. I'm talking as I pull up to the red light, and I saw what looked like a large, winged being coming in like it was either landing behind the building or landing basically on top of it."

The reason he described it as landing, he said, was because "it was coming down, and it looked like it had its chest out with its wings flared up like it was trying to slow down enough to come in for a landing."

Manuel responded to what he was seeing in what I felt was a very normal, credible way; he started yelling.

"I remember yelling out to my wife 'What the hell is that?' She's like 'What? What? What?' I told her what I was seeing," he told me. "She said it could be a goose, and I said, 'This is way larger than a goose.' I've seen geese. Right now, I see geese all over the place here. There are geese everywhere. They're migrating."

According to Manuel, he was sitting in the third lane of traffic near the intersection when movement caught his eye. That's when he looked over and saw the creature.

"The street at the traffic stop is five lanes, and it was rush hour, so slamming on the brakes and trying to get a good look was an invitation to get into a wreck," he said. "I found a place to turn around and went back, drove around a few places. I couldn't get onto their property, because it's sealed off. It's an old building, and I guess they're using it for storage now. At least one of the garages is used for storage of compressors or something, because there was an open garage and I could see inside, and there were mobile compressors. Last thing I needed was to have airport security all over me for trespassing. So, I drove around, and at one point there was an opening where I could go in. I went in, took a few pictures, and quickly got out, trying to find this thing, and I wasn't able to find it."

Manuel said that the creature had "membranous wings" with "no feathers."

"Honestly, this did not look like a goose," he said. "It was brownish/grayish, more on the brownish side, and it didn't look as big—it's not like some of the reports we've taken since we started investigating—this thing wasn't six or seven feet tall; it was maybe, at best, four feet tall. The wings were membranous. The only way I can describe them, the only

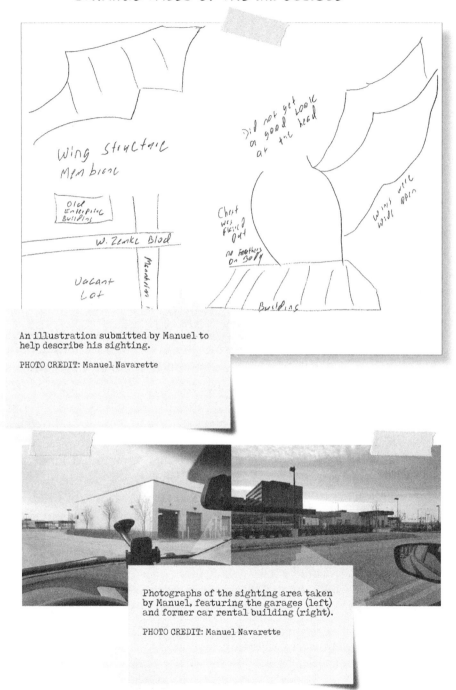

An illustration submitted by Manuel to help describe his sighting.

PHOTO CREDIT: Manuel Navarette

Photographs of the sighting area taken by Manuel, featuring the garages (left) and former car rental building (right).

PHOTO CREDIT: Manuel Navarette

thing I could compare them to, they kind of looked like an imp's wings. I never got a really good look at the head. The sighting itself only lasted one, maybe two seconds."

However, he continued, "I know it only lasted two seconds, but you're able to get a lot of information in those two seconds. I can honestly tell you that it had no feathers. It looked like it had no feathers on it, just membranous wings. It was far larger than what a Canadian goose is. Its legs were tucked up beneath it, because it looked like it was coming in to land either on top of or behind the building. What I saw was basically the chest and the wings. What I got a good look at was the wings—they were completely outspread. It looked like it was trying to spread itself out so it could slow down for a landing."

It seemed unlikely to me that Manuel had misidentified a bird, even my favorite go-to for misidentifications, the majestic great blue heron. At that distance, with the level of detail he was able to give, him getting it that wrong just didn't add up to me, at least not without some other evidence to back it up. If we had a photograph to work from, then maybe we could have made a determination one way or another, but in this case, I opted to do what I always do in this situation: continue as though what the witness is saying is true, unless I have verifiable evidence to the contrary.

Manuel continues to actively investigate in and around the area, but to-date, he has yet to see the creature again, whatever it was.

More than anything, Manuel's experience sounded like one of the pterosaur reports we receive from time to time.

In August of 2019, The Singular Fortean Society received a report from a witness, Diniah, who said she and her family had seen a pterosaur like one reported in Wheaton, Illinois earlier that year. Diniah, her mother Gloria, and father Darnell all saw the creature just outside of Pine Bluff, Arkansas in February of 2017.

"I read your article on the sighting of the pterosaur, and I would like to share my story on when me and my family saw the exact same thing a year and a half ago in Arkansas, entering in the town of Pine Bluff," reported Diniah in an email.

We were trying to take a short cut to Pine Bluff for a funeral, so we took a back road. My mother was sleeping, and I was on my phone; my father was driving. As he was driving, he saw something, at first, he thought it was a bird, but he had never seen a bird with that long of a wingspan and a long tail.

As it got closer, he yelled at me and my mother to look in the sky. We looked and I said, "OMG WHAT IS THAT."

My mother was in shock, and me and my father said it looked like it was in the family of a dinosaur...We continued driving, still in awe, as it flew slow into the trees with its long wingspan. We went home and researched it, but they're supposed to be extinct, right? Nope. We knew we weren't crazy! My father looked at it for a long time before telling me and my mother to look up, and he's definitely not crazy.

I contacted Diniah to ask for more details, including the date and time of their encounter, and anything she could remember of the creature's appearance.

The date was Friday, February 3rd, 2017, in the evening—after 5 p.m., around dusk. The best way I can describe the creature is like a pterodactyl with a long tail. The wingspan looked 30 feet, according to my father, but he said that's just how it looked. I'm not sure, really, how long it was, only because we looked from the angle of a car. [I] just know it was very long.

It was definitely bigger than a human and bigger than the car we were in, which was a full-size sedan. Its size was intimidating. Just to give you an image, it was like seeing something out of Jurassic Park.

I remember the creature was probably black, and when it was flying it flew slow, not like a bird. Its wings were so big, I think that was the reason for it flying the way it did. We had to keep driving to Pine Bluff and couldn't stop in traffic because back roads are narrow, and we already had traffic behind us because we slowed down to look at the creature.

I was also able to contact Gloria and Darnell, who agreed to recount the sighting as they remembered it.

"The bird I saw was a very large bird, about 30 feet across," said Darnell.

The creature was low-flying and seemed to be moving as if it was cruising. I saw it as I was driving on a detoured route in Arkansas.

At first, I thought it was a shadow crossing over the car, I looked up through the sunroof and wasn't sure if I really saw it. I squinted my eyes to refocus and make sure I wasn't seeing something that couldn't be there.

I called out to my wife and daughter to look; they both saw it too. The creature looked like a pterodactyl at first, I know that couldn't be possible. I thought to myself, maybe it's a drone, remote-controlled device or something man-made. We were wondering what could it be?

When they returned home to Chicago, Illinois, the family couldn't help but tell others about what they had seen.

"I mentioned it to my brother-in-law after arriving back home to Chicago and left it alone. I knew that I saw something out of the ordinary but didn't quite know what to do or where to go with the sighting," said Darnell.

Unfortunately, the experience of sharing such a sighting isn't always positive.

"When we got back to Chicago is when we told people like friends and family—even a doctor," Diniah said. "We told a bunch of people hoping we weren't the only ones who saw this...When we told people back in Chicago, they didn't believe us."

It wasn't until they saw the sighting report out of Wheaton that was published in July that they felt relief; somebody else had seen the same thing.

"I wondered about it from time to time and just threw it in the back of my mind, until I stumbled across an article on my phone about a sighting in Wheaton, Illinois, and I became excited all over again, feeling relieved that someone else had seen the creature too," Darnell said. "I knew it was really what I saw that evening. I'll never forget it, especially now that others have seen it also."

Pine Bluff is the tenth largest city in Arkansas, with a population of almost 43,000. It is surrounded by natural areas, with the easternmost border of the Ouachita National Forest lying around 60 miles to its northwest. The Ouachita National Forest, known among forteans for its Bigfoot sightings, is nearly 3,000 square miles of wilderness that sprawls over western Arkansas and portions of eastern Oklahoma.

Wheaton, a suburban city on the western edge of the greater Chicago metropolitan area, is of a similar size and composition. Contrary to what one might expect, the area around Chicago is full of parks, forest preserves, and other natural areas. If you're going to see an impossible animal somewhere, seems like it's as likely to be in liminal spaces like these as it is to be anywhere else.

In July of 2019, Lon spoke to a man who said he'd seen a "pterosaur" in the late afternoon of July 5th.

"I received a telephone call from a witness...who described the sighting of a cryptid winged creature," said Lon of the report.

[The witness] was driving on Jewell Road, about a half mile west of Gary Avenue in Wheaton, Illinois, during the late afternoon of July 5th, 2019. He had been helping a friend with a yard sale.

As [he] was looking ahead of him, he noticed a strange form flying in the sky at an altitude of approximately 200 feet. The profile was that of a pterosaur, in particular the long tail with a 'spade' on the end. The head was indistinguishable because of the angle, but the wings were wide and similar to the classic form. The creature was dark in color and propelled itself with slow, deliberate wing flaps.

[The witness] was able to observe the winged creature for 15-20 second and is positive that it was not a crane or heron, with which he is very familiar. The wingspan was undetermined, but much wider than any known indigenous bird.

"This is a continuation of cryptid bird and winged humanoid sightings in the Upper Midwest, in particular throughout the state of Illinois and Indiana," added Lon.

It was, indeed. We've been receiving reports of strange flying creatures—from humanoids to pterosaurs—around Lake Michigan and the states surrounding it for years. Most of those sightings and the investigation into them were recorded in The Lake Michigan Mothman: High Strangeness in the Midwest. Anything not included in that book is in this one, at least of the sightings Emily and I have personally investigated so far, and while a few of the previous reports are referenced in this work, I've tried not to create too much overlap.

Still, one does measure a circle beginning anywhere, and noting the interconnectedness of these phenomena can leave us feeling at times like a dog chasing their own tail. The sightings we investigate lead to more, seemingly endlessly, and so we find ourselves constantly revisiting those with which we assumed we were done. The lessons here are 1. don't assume, and 2. we're never done.

CHAPTER 9

NO LAUGHING MATTER

Those feelings of dread and evil Daniel mentioned were something I've heard from multiple witnesses. They're not always mentioned together, but people often mention at least one of them, especially when it comes to winged humanoids. And of course, encountering them at home only makes it worse. At the time of Daniel's sighting, I was most reminded of the experience of Paula, a woman who said she had seen a hulking, winged creature in Wauconda, Illinois. That encounter was preceded by a sighting of a strange beam of light three years prior.

On April 20th, 2014, Paula was sitting near a window in the bedroom of her ground-level apartment near the Lakewood Forest Preserve in Wauconda when she saw a bright beam of light "come shooting down" across the street at around 11 p.m.

"It was so bright and defined," Paula told me during a phone interview.

The light, which lasted between 15 and 20 seconds, was an orange/gold color and did not illuminate its surroundings; nor did it move much, making only a slight "side-to-side or back-and-forth" motion.

The light retracted at one point, only to reappear a moment later.

Paula fell back onto her bed in shock.

"Oh my god, this thing sees me!" she remembered thinking. "I had the deepest feeling this thing saw me, it knows."

But the light retracted a final time and was gone.

"I heard a hum at the end, just before it took off," said Paula.

Three years later, on April 17th, 2017, Paula encountered a terrifying winged being in the same area. She was taking the garbage out just before 6 a.m. when something drew her eye from across the street. In the early morning gloom, she saw a huge, winged being.

Paula described the being as perhaps seven to eight feet tall when standing erect, but it carried itself hunched over, limping along. It was completely black, and from what she could see its upper body and head were covered in hair. The being had long, leathery wings which were

The beam of light appeared between the two buildings shown, in front of the tree, and did not disturb its surroundings. ˣ[Everything] was very still,ˣ said Paula.

PHOTO CREDIT: Paula

The creature was between the sidewalk and where Paula had seen the strange beam of light two years before.

PHOTO CREDIT: Paula

partially wrapped around its body as it moved towards Paula, jumping forward similarly to someone moving through a strobe light. The horrific creature made an unnatural groaning noise as it advanced.

Paula felt a palpable sense of evil emanating from the bat-winged monster.

"This is evil," she recalled. "I'm seeing evil."

Fearing for her safety, she quickly turned to flee back into her apartment. After fumbling with her keys for a moment, she opened the door and turned around, terrified that the creature might be right behind her—but it was gone.

Paula said that she only knew a few of her neighbors personally, and unfortunately the ones she knew had not witnessed either event, although one of her neighbors with whom she was friends did take her encounters seriously.

"I don't know what to say," Paula said of her experiences. "But I know what I saw."

Paula certainly isn't the only witness who has related these kinds of experiences happening at or near their home.

The Singular Fortean Society was contacted in February of 2020 by 60-year-old California resident Richard Polk, who said that on a foggy night in the fall of 2009 he had an unusual run-in with a winged humanoid in La Habra.

Historical weather data showed that there was a possibility of fog in the area on the night of Richard's sighting, formed by high humidity and the ground cooling to near the dew point after sunset in calm conditions with a clear sky.

I was able to speak with Richard over the phone about his experience.

"I went to a Halloween party, it was Halloween night, and by the time I got home it was around 11 p.m. I was down at a friend's house until maybe 1 a.m., and I came out and as I was walking towards my house I was on the left side of the street," Richard said. "From there, I walked down the street about maybe 150 yards all the way to the other side of the T cul-de-sac—when you come in you've got to go left or right and they're both dead ends. As I was walking, I got to the part where the T comes in from the road. That only left me another 50 yards until my apartment. As I'm walking, I hear a ticking, like tick-tick-tick-tick, fast; it was something that was moving."

He heard it before he saw it, due to the thick fog that night, but soon enough the creature was running past him.

"As I was walking on the sidewalk, I looked over to see what it was, and at first glimpse, all I caught was pretty much just feathers—I couldn't see the face," Richard explained. "It was probably only 15 feet away from me. I was on the sidewalk, and there's maybe three feet of grass, the curb, and then there were parked cars. It was running maybe five feet from the cars, down the opposite way. The first glimpse I got was in-between the cars, and as I'm looking to the right, it went past the rear of an older station wagon [with large wraparound windows], and my second glimpse of it was of basically the legs up to about maybe the stomach, not quite all of the feet but I could see the calves and the thighs. It was not even four feet tall, at the most. As I get the second glimpse of this thing, right away I'm like 'What the heck?' I came around in-between the cars and it's past me, then, and I look back down the street and that's when I saw this thing go running away. When I was standing on the sidewalk looking through the windows of the station wagon, I couldn't even see its head, so I was thinking a bird of some kind, maybe a roadrunner or a peacock or something."

But it didn't take him long to discern this was no bird—at least not one he'd ever seen. This creature used plantigrade locomotion, like a human.

"I've done a lot of hunting, and I know my birds," Richard explained. "I know what birds are about and how they run. The thing's thigh was the size of an average human man's thigh, but muscled, and the calf was the same way. Its feet were the size of a human man's hand, at least. It had three claws, I recall, but they were very strange looking. There was no hair on the legs, but they looked pock-marked and there were long, single hairs here and there. It was just a quick glance, but the vision in my mind of the legs is so vivid."

"As it ran away, I could see wings that came down almost to the ground," he continued. "I never really saw the face. But when it ran between the cars, I remember thinking 'I didn't even see a beak.' If it was a bird, it would have had a beak; I would have been able to see a beak. It had hair like a troll doll, that went up and then down, it was pure white. I couldn't really make out [its wings] until I got between the cars and saw it running, they were feathered. The wings came down, they were big wings. The hair came straight up and then back, all the way around. And the face—there was hair in the way."

121

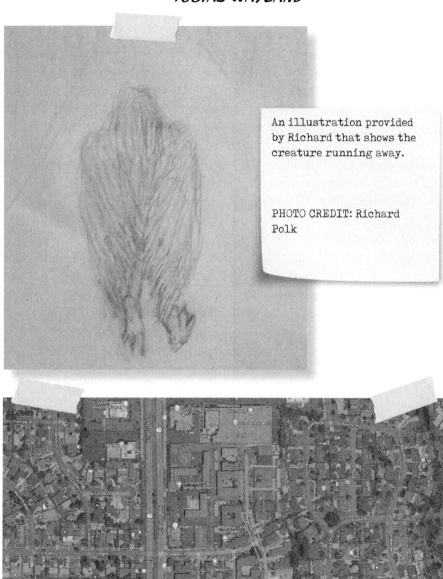

An illustration provided by Richard that shows the creature running away.

PHOTO CREDIT: Richard Polk

The rectangle represents the approximate area of missing fog, while the red arrow indicates the direction Richard was walking and the approximate location of the sighting, which took place just past the T intersection. The creature was running north, the opposite direction of Richard.

Richard watched the creature as it ran through an area of the street conspicuously absent of fog before vanishing into the night.

"This fog had maybe 75 yards to 100 yards of open space, but otherwise I couldn't see the sidewalk on the other side. I couldn't see my house. The streetlights were lit up, there were two or three street-lights. But the middle of the street was all lit up. This is a regular-sized, residential street," he said. "That's when I realized it was all open in the street. But I couldn't see past the sidewalk on the other side—I couldn't see anything. I was only 50 yards from my apartment, and I couldn't even see that. When I turned around to look at it, it ran into the fog and disappeared."

According to Richard, the entire encounter lasted maybe 10 seconds, but it was the most scared he'd ever been.

"By the time I got between the cars and looked back, it was already 20 yards away and running. I wanted so bad to say something, but I couldn't. I was just too scared; the hair on the back of my neck and head was standing up, and I have the feeling that I'm glad I didn't," he said. "It was almost an evil presence."

Richard was so frightened by the encounter, he said, that "I ran to my apartment, got inside, turned all the lights off, got into my big, master closet, opened up a sleeping bag and slept in there that night. I was scared to death. I was the only one in the apartment."

Despite having gone to a Halloween party that night, Richard insisted that he was sober.

Ultimately, he has a feeling that he might have gotten lucky in his encounter, explaining "It was foggy, I mean I couldn't even see the [sidewalk across the street], so maybe that's why it couldn't see me."

Richard also related a series of strange sightings had by a friend in the area.

"A month or so before this happened, a friend of mine who lived there told me that in the backyard she'd had multiple sightings of something with red eyes that glowed. I didn't think too much about it, I thought maybe it was raccoons or something," he said.

As for his own sighting, Richard said he's "never seen anything like it," and that he had looked for an explanation for years before finding The Singular Fortean Society.

"The closest thing I could ever come up with was the Moth-man," he said.

The month prior to speaking with Richard, in January of 2020, I interviewed a woman who wished to report her 2001 sighting of four winged humanoids in Berwyn, Illinois. The witness said that she was directed by one of her sons to view the Small Town Monsters documentary Terror in the Skies, and after watching the 'Chicago Mothman' portion of the film, decided she wanted to disclose her sighting to me.

She initially contacted me via Facebook messenger, where I was able to schedule a phone interview.

"In 2001, we were in my backyard in Berwyn, which is next to Cicero, just outside of Chicago. We were having a picnic in the backyard. It was about nine or ten o'clock at night. Now, it scares me to talk about this, because I don't want to bring bad juju on myself," she told me over the phone.

I was in the backyard cleaning up and I look up in the air—it was a beautiful, moonlit night, just a couple days before 9/11—and the moon's out but it's kind of cloudy, I've got tiki torches in the backyard and those really big balls that light up like half a block.

I'm by myself, outside, cleaning and gathering stuff off of the table, and I see four humongous—they looked humongous—people, they looked like men, and they were all black and they had big wings, I mean HUGE wings. The wings were not feathery, they were bat wings or demon wings. I looked at them and there were four in a row, and they looked like they were standing up [horizontally] as they flew. They were muscular, they were big, and I looked up and went "Oh my God, what the fuck is that?"

The woman offered that she's "sensitive," in the sense of having a natural affinity for psychic phenomena.

"I've got these weird gifts and they've always been scary to me; I never understood them," she said. "I found out after years of therapy and talking to priests that I'm blessed, and you can either learn to use it or suppress it. I chose to suppress it, because it's scary."

That sensitivity, and her reaction to it, might help explain what came next.

"They didn't hear me, they were too high up to hear me, but two of them looked directly at me, and when they looked at me, they had red eyes," she said. "I freaked out, because they looked directly into my eyes. I ran into my house, and I was starting to cry because I was freaking out. My cousin, who has since passed away, said 'What's wrong? What happened? What's the matter?' But I was too afraid to speak; I just wanted to go back outside to make sure they were gone. I went out there and they were gone. They never came back. I was afraid for weeks after that to go outside."

Like many witnesses, she shared her experience with a few people, only to be mocked. Still, she stands by her story.

"This was not my imagination. I don't do drugs and I don't drink. This blew my mind; completely blew my mind. I told some people at work, but of course they laughed at me. They taunted me; thought I was crazy. To this day, I know what I saw. I won't let anyone try to manipulate my story or tell me I was hallucinating," she said.

Several years ago, over a decade after the sighting, one of her sons mentioned to her the significance of the date and its proximity to the national tragedy of 9/11.

The woman's testimony and corresponding weather data tentatively indicate the night of the sighting to be September 8th, three days before the terrorist attacks.

My son, who's 32, said to me "Mom, this is really odd, but did you ever think that 9/11 happened right after you saw [those winged creatures]?"

I said, "No, I never thought of that."

He said, "You saw four of them, right?"

I said, "Yeah."

He said, "Right in front of each other like perfectly aligned, and they were huge with humongous wings. They were out to do something; you could tell they were on a mission. You got the [Twin Towers of the World Trade Center], you've got [the Pentagon], and you've got [Flight 93] that crashed in a field."

I said, "Oh my God, I never thought of that. I never ever thought of that."

As I've said before, I don't believe there's any connection between winged humanoid sightings and disasters, but regardless of the veracity of that perceived connection, the effect this experience had on the woman with whom I spoke is undeniable.

"I never even knew Mothman existed, never heard any of the stories," she said. "There's a lot of stuff that I never dabbled in, ever.

Which is scary, because you've got nobody to talk to, and you're afraid to talk to people. You're afraid to say what you've seen. I never called the police; I was so scared."

I wish her experience was unique, but the fact is, most people with whom I speak don't talk much about their sighting until they meet me. Normally, after their experience, which is often very impactful, maybe even traumatic, they want to talk about it. They will turn to a loved one, could be a family member or a close friend, and that person whom they trust and hoped to confide in laughs at them. It's enough for most people to never speak of their experience again, until they're watching a Small Town Monsters documentary or come across an article published by The Singular Fortean Society and discover that yes, other people are reporting similar events and yes, there are people who will take them seriously and treat them with respect.

I was contacted by Jonathan Lane, a 21-year-old resident of Rockford, Illinois, in October of 2020. The young man wished to report a sighting of what he would later describe as a "giant, shapeless, black thing" with "two very large red eyes."

According to Jonathan, the sighting took place between 10:20 and 10:30 p.m. on an August night in 2016, sometime "before school had started that year."

It was very late at night—my mother works nights because she's a nurse—so I walk her to her car every night. I walked her out to her car, and she got in it and left. Then, as I'm walking up to the house, I hear a noise that's like screeching brakes or something and I instantly look up.

There's a big tree in our yard and I see this giant, shapeless, black thing—and it has two very large red eyes. As soon as I made eye contact with it, it made that sound again. Instantly, it fills me with fear and intimidation, and I run in the house and start freaking out. The sound was so weird. I can still hear it clearly in my head. Like a large bird's caw. Reminds me of the dinosaurs from Jurassic Park, like the velociraptors.

The next day or so, when it was light, I went outside, and I looked where the branch was and tried to see where I'd seen the top of it and where the blackness was compared to the tree. It was pretty substantial. It would have to be nine feet tall. It was a large space. The wingspan just faded into the darkness around it.

A photo taken by Jonathan, showing the area of his sighting and the being's approximate height.

PHOTO CREDIT: Jonathan Lane

It was shapeless, but where the eyes were, I did see a little notch above its head where I could see sky. What really bothered me was the red eyes and how far apart they were. It showed just how large it was.

Like many witnesses, Jonathan was met with ridicule when he initially shared his story and kept it quiet for years afterward, at least until he saw *Terror in the Skies.*

"My father was there, and I told him about it, and he started laughing and making fun of me," he explained. "So, since then I've just kept [my experience] very private, [although] I told my sister about it once. I've just never really forgotten about it. I never knew what it was. I saw the documentary [*Terror in the Skies*] and it was just mind-blowing to see you guys talk about stuff like that. I just wanted to reach out somehow."

I'm glad he did. It means a lot to me that any of the work we do can give someone the kind of relief I'd yearned for when I was younger. It's why I do what I do.

Like Paula and Gerald, the weird events at Jonathan's house didn't end with a single creature sighting.

Approximately a year after his sighting of the red-eyed entity, Jonathan said he saw an unidentified flying object in the same area.

I was driving home with a friend of mine from work, and we were almost to my house. [We were] in the same [area as the winged entity sighting]—there are a lot of trees and there's only a little section of the sky that's open right by my house, and that's where the big tree is where the [previous] incident happened. It was the same part of the sky.

I'm not claiming it was anything specific, but I saw a very prominent UFO. Very large, very prominent. I had my friend stop the car and we got out. I just don't know what it was. It was clear enough where I could see panels, like windows. It was very scary. My friend, she's a bit younger than me, she got very scared, so we had to leave.

Whatever that was, it was not normal. It was shaped like a pear. It had probably a hundred windows all over it. It was lit up. It was very weird how it was lit up. The whole thing was illuminated, but it had lines of light—almost like waves of light going through it. It's hard to explain. It almost looked like it had white light stripes through it, but it was an undulating movement. The very top of it was black, and the very bottom of it was black, but the center was illuminated. I could see where it was being lit up and it was like miniature squares making up the whole object.

Whatever he saw, Jonathan's sightings have definitely had an effect on him.

"Both of those things very much bothered me," he said. "We have a huge picture window in our living room and it's a huge pet peeve of mine to make sure those curtains are closed, overlapping, so nothing shows at night. I had a room in the corner of the house nearby that tree, and eventually I had to move rooms."

He added that, despite his fear of doing so, it felt refreshing to express his experiences to someone, and that his "main motivation for sharing [them was] to add credibility and make it easier for other people to come forward."

I respect that. Destigmatizing these experiences is an uphill battle, but it's one worth fighting, and every one of these reports that we can present authentically for review gets us a little closer to victory.

These experiences have a real effect on people, sometimes even entire families, the echoes of which reverberate across generations.

In May of 2020, our friend Adam Benedict referred a woman named Selina to The Singular Fortean Society. She said she was looking for "assistance on finding answers to an incident my mom and I had happen about 20 years ago."

Her initial report came via email.

Back in December of 2001, our apartment completely burned down, and we lost everything. The company my father worked for ended up paying for a fully furnished apartment until ours was rebuilt. At this point in time, we lived in Madison, Wisconsin—more specifically, on Allied Drive. But that place burned down, so we were sent to a place right off of the Seminole Highway exit off of the [Beltline Highway.]

In January of 2002, about two weeks after our fire, my mom got off at our exit, and turned left. As we were coming up to the second set of lights, my mom saw what she believed to be a "large bat-like creature." She said that it was very opaque in color (details were harder to make out because it was evening when this happened), it was very large, and she said that as she turned her head to look at this thing, it turned and looked at her. She believes she made direct eye contact with it. Its eyes were glowing red, and the face was very bat-like from what she could see. It was flying, but it wasn't flapping its wings like a normal bat would, instead it was almost gliding, kind of. I don't know how else to explain it. It had been flying the opposite direction that we were going. She tried to get a better look, but it was gone as soon as it appeared.

I was in the car when this happened. I didn't see what she did, but I do remember my mom screaming and panicking.

A few weeks had gone by, and we were back in our original apartment. Our basement had one laundry machine and one dryer that I can remember, and it was directly across from OUR storage unit.

After moving back into the rebuilt apartment, my mom decided she was going to do laundry and went downstairs. As she was doing the laundry though, for whatever reason, she decided to turn around and look into our storage unit. After a minute, she noticed something at the very back wall behind all of our junk. As she focused more on what exactly she was seeing, she *BELIEVES* she saw the very same creature. She saw a large bat-like face, with the same red, glowing eyes. She said it had been staring back at her.

She completely panicked and ran as fast as she could back upstairs, and she NEVER went back down there again. We moved out of there soon after that happened.

About two or three days after her second incident with seeing this creature, she said she saw a few news reports on sightings of a creature very similar to what she had seen.

My mom and I over the years have done our best to do research into this, and we have tried VERY hard to find these articles and reports on these sightings, but for whatever reason, it seems like they were completely removed. Almost as if no one wants these reports going public.

I stumbled across something Adam had posted and had a feeling he would be able to assist me in finding answers. My mom almost never talks about it because people never believe her. But we KNOW what happened and we know we weren't the only ones. But we can't seem to find anything regarding this.

Emily and I lived in Madison at the time, and I'm familiar with the area Selina said her mother had first seen the creature. Seminole Highway skirts the western edge of the University of Wisconsin-Madison Arboretum, a 1,260-acre ecological restoration site a few miles outside of campus, although still firmly within the city. It's covered in thick deciduous and coniferous forests, occasionally broken by prairies and wetlands. If I was going to hide a monster in Madison, that's where I'd do it.

Not long after Adam referred her to us, I was able to speak with Selina over the phone regarding the incident. She said that she had previously been given permission to use her mother's first name, Heather, in the report.

"I was six years old at the time," Selina recalled. "My mom was the one who witnessed everything firsthand, I just remember the fear and the paranoia when she saw what she saw in the basement. I mean, she never set foot in the basement again, she wouldn't even go and stand on the stairwell. I remember some people in my family would sit there and kind of make fun of her, and some of them didn't believe her. They'd say 'Hey, Heather, go grab the sled from the storage unit.' Mom would just look at them, say 'No,' and walk away. Everyone thought it was the funniest thing, but it traumatized my mom to this day. She'll bring it up occasionally, but she doesn't talk about it that much because most people don't believe her."

Although, Selina said, "I think my dad believed her, honestly."

Despite her age at the time of the sightings, I asked Selina to recall everything she could about the encounters.

"The first time that she saw it, we were on the bridge by the [Seminole Highway] exit," she said. "If I remember correctly, I had a toy or was drinking a drink or something—my attention was down towards the floor—and I just remember the car kind of slowed down pretty drastically and my mom screamed and she said, 'What the [fuck] was that?' She freaked out, and when I looked up, I saw her head was turned and she looked like she'd seen a ghost. She didn't tell me what she saw right away, she was just in shock. She was paranoid to drive at night for a bit after that. That happened, when she saw the thing on the bridge, that would have been early to mid-January of 2002—right after our apartment fire."

Her mother's next encounter happened soon after.

"A few weeks later was when she saw it in the storage unit in our apartment," Selina continued. "The apartment had been restored and we were able to move back in. My mom had gone downstairs to do the laundry, and I don't remember if she told me that she had this feeling that she had to look or if she just wanted to look, I don't really know why she looked behind her in the storage unit, but she did, and after a minute, she noticed a face; when she looked closer, she said that it looked almost exactly like the face of the thing that she said she had seen on the bridge."

"What really got to her were the red eyes," she added. "[My mother] said, to this day, the red eyes that she saw are burned in her memory. She will never forget the look in the eyes, and she said that it's just something she'll never forget. The eyes are what really terrified her."

When I asked if they'd experienced anything that might be considered paranormal in the apartment other than Heather's encounter, Selina responded that "almost everyone in that building who was open to [the paranormal] really thought the building was haunted."

"I do remember a few instances where we would hear a baby crying. At the time, my brother was an infant, so my parents would go to check on him and he would be dead asleep, and they would still hear a baby crying. It was constant, it was almost nonstop," she said. "Some nights, they would hear all of the dishes flying out of the cabinets and crashing on the floor, and they would think that we had an intruder, and everything was untouched—it was like nothing even happened."

But, she said, "The activity really started getting worse when the basement started getting redone, because they were doing something in the basement. The activity started picking up after that. The apartment fire happened soon after."

The activity continued after the restoration with another concerning incident involving fire.

"I remember, soon after the building itself was rebuilt after the fire, my aunt and uncle had been living in the upstairs unit above us, and I remember being up in their apartment once and my aunt was braiding my hair, and I went downstairs because she was going to jump in the shower," Selina said. "They always had a decorative candle on their table—my family is Mexican, so they had those religious decorative candles—and they had one in the center of their coffee table. They didn't really light them up at that point in time, they never had a reason to, and so like I said, I went downstairs, my aunt was in the shower, my uncle was in the bedroom, and when my aunt got out of the shower, she noticed that the entire apartment was full of smoke. She thought, 'Oh my God, there's another fire.' It was the candle. The candle itself had set on fire—it wasn't lit, it had just set on fire. It was in the center of the table, and it even left a charred circle where it had been."

The events were very impactful on Selina and her mother, and they still periodically revisit the topic.

"Me and my mom, over the years, whenever we do bring it up, we do our best to look into it. We've just never really gotten anywhere. This time around, I was really determined to find something. I didn't know what I was looking for, I just know that to this day it really bothers my mom and I want to try to get her some type of answers," she said.

We talked about the similarities between her family's experiences and other high strangeness reports—that phantom baby crying popped up frequently during the Point Pleasant Mothman sightings back in the '60s—and I sent Selina a link to our timeline of Lake Michigan Mothman reports, and asked that she have her mother contact me with any questions or concerns. I never heard back, although that's not particularly unusual.

A lot of people find that they're more comfortable moving on from an event like this once they've put it out there, especially once it becomes evident that the harder you look at these phenomena, the more questions you're left with. Hard answers are in short supply. Commonalities, however, are abundant. For instance, many witnesses find themselves afflicted with strange phenomena before or after creature sightings.

The Singular Fortean Society was contacted by email in September of 2019 by a woman who said that she and her son had an encounter with a mysterious winged humanoid in May of that year outside of Parsonsburg, Maryland.

My son, who is 15, and I were driving home from the store late one night at the beginning of the summer. We live in Parsonsburg, Maryland, a tiny town. We saw something crouched by the side of a bendy, woodsy back road, with a neighborhood and pond close by. My initial thought was that it was a bird, and that it was going to hit my car. When it flew up it appeared to be a dark grey human about six feet or taller, with smooth skin and bat-like wings. It had human feet, which we clearly saw as it shot up and over the trees, sort of gliding. We were stunned. We asked each other what the hell we saw, and then didn't speak of it again for quite some time.

I contacted the woman via telephone, and she agreed to the use of her first name, Bobbi. We both decided that it was best for her son to remain completely anonymous.

"We had gone to Walmart on a Friday night. We're night owls, so we always do late-night 'Oh, let's run here, let's run there,'" Bobbi said. "It was probably between midnight and 1 a.m. We were on Dagsboro Road, and it cuts from town to the country, basically. We live in Parsonsburg, and Walmart is in Salisbury. It's a very winding road, like very, very twisty."

Bobbi wasn't sure of the exact date of their sighting but was reasonably sure it was in the latter half of May. She described weather conditions that evening as clear and bright, and historical weather data confirmed both Friday the 17th and 24th would match that description.

She was driving with her son in the passenger seat, and was only going about 30 mph. As she rounded one of the road's many curves, Bobbi said she saw something only 20 feet or so ahead in the road.

"It was crouched, and I had a couple thoughts: the first one was 'It's going to hit my car,' then the second thought was 'What the hell kind of bird is that out here at one o'clock in the morning?' Then, when I got closer, I saw that it didn't look like a bird, its skin was smooth, and my brain wasn't registering it at all. By the time I was on it, it had started to stand up and was probably six feet tall, at least," said Bobbi.

Bobbi's mind reeled at the seemingly impossible situation unfolding before her.

"It was big, you know? I was sure it was going to hit the front of my car or something. So, I slowed down a little more and kept going, and as I got closer to it, it started to move, and I guess I was just staring at it, and it seemed to be crouched down—like a buzzard or something. When it raised up, I didn't see anything on the road, I didn't see anything that it was crouched eating, like a buzzard would. It lifted itself up, and I honestly to this day cannot even tell you what I saw, until it reached the tip of my windshield. I still was thinking 'This thing is going to hit my car!' Then, as it went up, and fully stretched its body out, I could see that it was very grey and very smooth in appearance, like it would be smooth if I touched it. It was bald, it was bald-headed, and I saw feet, but like human feet," she said. "Like grey human feet."

Bobbi explained that the creature "was crouched on the left side of the road. It went up straight and then over across to the right where my son was and then up over the trees on that side. He saw the front from a side angle as it flew over us. The last thing we saw was the feet. And then he was just gone. We didn't see him glide over the trees; he was just gone."

"It seemed to be very, very bald. The top of the head was bald. It was very round and very bald. There were ears. I thought it was a human head," she added.

According to her son, who had seen more of the creature's face, it "looked like a skull, with sunken eyes, and with skin over it."

It took Bobbi a moment to react before she looked to her son for confirmation of what she'd seen.

"I just stared; I really didn't process what I was seeing. It flew straight up in front of my car, and when its feet were up above my car is when I was like 'holy shit!' It went up over the trees, it never flapped its wings—it just kind of glided up off the ground. I waited for a second, and then I looked at my son and I asked 'Did you see that? Am I crazy?' His face was completely still. He had no expression, and all he said to me was 'I saw bat wings and human feet.' And then, we didn't say another word about it," she said.

Both Bobbi and her son seemingly forgot about the event completely until several weeks later when they were driving down the same stretch of road at night.

"We drove home in a stunned daze, and we didn't say anything else," she explained. "And then a couple of weeks later we were driving down that road again and I said [to my son] 'Oh my god, do you remember what we saw?' And he said, 'Yes, oh my god!'"

The two searched online but couldn't find anything like what they'd seen—until Bobbi's son came across a video about Mothman on YouTube.

"He found some stuff on the Mothman. We started googling Mothman stories, and that's when we came across [The Singular Fortean Society]," she said.

Bobbi was struck by the number of sighting reports like their own.

"That's when I was like 'holy crap!' Because when I saw the sketches [by Donie Odulio] that were on one of the stories, it matched to a 'T' [what we had seen]. Besides the eyes, we didn't see any red eyes, but I didn't really see any specific features. My son said he saw the face, and he said 'No, the eyes were just kind of sunk in,' and he said he saw wings and hands," she explained.

Although her son said he has a strong feeling of fear associated with the encounter, Bobbi said she didn't experience any overpowering emotions, other than bewilderment at how they so suddenly and mysteriously forgot the event.

"We're very talkative, and we love creepy stuff, but we'd never seen anything," she said. "That's what threw me for a loop, because we literally just drove home after in silence. I didn't wake up the next day and tell a single soul. I didn't even remember it until we drove back down that road."

Following the event, the family experienced one incident of a potentially psychic phenomenon which I had to promise not to share, and in addition, according to Bobbi, their "kitchen radio turns on by itself all the time." The radio was purchased before the incident and has no prior history of malfunction.

Both Bobbi and her son are otherwise handling their experience well, and more than anything are relieved to find that they aren't alone.

"Other people have seen this," Bobbi said. "We're not crazy."

After speaking with her, I can tell you that Bobbi didn't seem crazy to me; at least no more than the rest of us.

That's something that has always struck me. The people who report these events come from every stratum of society; they might be your coworker, attend your church, or coach your kid's little league team. If you passed any of these witnesses on the street, you wouldn't give them a second glance. In short, they're not crazy and they're not making it up.

CHAPTER 10

WHEN GOD CLOSES A DOOR, HE OPENS A HIGH STRANGENESS WINDOW AREA

These phenomena have a way of sticking with people, whether in their psychological effect or their attachment to certain individuals, but sometimes, it seems like it's a place to which they've attached themselves. These places, when they're of the sufficient, arbitrarily decided size to be considered as such, are often referred to as "window areas," and if the phenomena present are weird enough, you might even find the words "high strangeness" in front.

Personally, I allow for the phrase high strangeness window area to be flexible enough to include something as small as a house, like the one Quinn grew up in, or those included in this chapter. It might be comforting for some to categorize certain things as haunted houses and others as window areas, but I don't find those contrived divisions to be helpful. The phenomena involved are too often the same to pretend as though it makes a difference how big the area is in which they keep repeating. Let's call a spade a spade and a window a window, regardless of how wide it opens.

In October of 2020, our friend Aubrey Bowen, a Georgia-based paranormal investigator, corresponded with a woman who claimed to have experienced a number of paranormal events between July and September of 2014 while working in an assisted living home.

Although Aubrey and I both verified the woman's identity and the location of the experiences, they're being kept private at the woman's request to protect those involved.

Aubrey first became aware of the events through a post on social media.

[I] worked at an assisted living home on the night shift. I lived in the basement apartment of the place and had a handheld camera walkie-talkie that could switch to see all the cameras. Mostly you just switched between cameras to make sure no one was wandering and only went upstairs if someone had fallen or gotten up. We were caring for this super tiny old woman. She was coming up on 100 [years old] and weighed like 60 [pounds]. She fell a lot, so it was easy for one person to pick her up and move her back in bed, it happened at least two times a week.

One night shift I was clicking through the cameras and saw what I thought was her standing in the hallway, it looked like a small, short person who was looking right at the door to her room just staring, not moving. As soon as I saw her standing in the hallway, I heard the sound of someone falling from upstairs. [I] ran up the stairs expecting to see her in the hallway, she wasn't there. She was in her room and had rolled off her bed. When I got her back into bed, she kept asking who was standing in the hallway. Noped out of that job a few weeks later because I hated how often people asked about someone who wasn't there, among other things.

In response to questions asked by Aubrey, the woman elaborated more on the unusual occurrences.

The residents always complained that time moved weird, like it was breakfast forever ago and they felt like they were being starved by the time next meal came. One of the old men complained that his shows would last too long and when he'd look at the clock no time had passed but he had been watching TV for hours. Weird stuff like that, we actually had to start setting timers for like every 10 minutes so everyone knew time was still passing because it would freak them out so badly. I never had any issues with that, so I figure it had to do with them being old—it was just a weird thing to have to do.

They would also complain someone would follow them around the halls. Mostly the women would complain about someone standing in their door watching them and they thought it was an employee, so they would make complaints about us staring at them from their doorway even though there was video proof that no one was doing that. It was a lot of weird things. Being in the basement was almost worse because every footstep or movement was super loud, and you really had to gauge if it was someone moving upstairs or if it was "nothing" or you'd spend all night running up and down the stairs for no reason. A few times it was things falling over or the piano slamming shut but for the most part it was never anything.

According to the woman, the assisted living home "was a regular house that they converted into a retirement home/care facility. It was constructed very oddly, but well, it was an entire two-story home but tacked on the back was another full sized three-bedroom home. The upstairs was the care facility, the basement was the employee living area and then through one more door in the basement was the other entire house. It was built around the 80's and then remodeled in like 2002 when my friend's dad bought it, which is when they added the house add-on and upgraded a lot and became a facility."

"It was in a residential area completely normal as far as anyone could tell. We did ask some of the neighbors if they had issues with anything weird and no one had anything to say," she added.

She concluded that she felt like "retirement homes just have a different energy stemming from the intention. Like they're being built to house people who are close to death, I feel like that alone could bring some weird energies into it. [I don't know], just a thought."

As for other members of the staff experiencing anything paranormal, she said "I know one other girl saw people in the cameras like I did, but everyone else just kind of ignored things like that. Everything was easily explained away to them. I don't believe they ever saw anything. The time thing was something everyone dealt with even if they didn't experience it directly, like I said we were having to set timers for the residents for almost every 10 minutes to reassure them time was still passing. I have never heard anyone anywhere ever experience the time thing, I've even tried to search it up as like just something older people experience or even something paranormal but never found anything."

Ultimately, the experiences had at the home are unlike any she's had before or since.

"I've had a few paranormal experiences before this that had to do with my grandma's house but nothing this extreme or severe," she said. "I'd never experienced anything like it before, especially with the time stuff."

In early March of 2021, Aubrey spoke to another woman—this time in Folkston, Georgia, less than 10 miles east of Okefenokee Swamp—who said that she and her family had experienced a series of paranormal events since moving into their home on Little Phoebe

Church Road in April of 2016.

"We are on Little Phoebe Church Road, which is just up from the Okefenokee refuge—the wildlife refuge. I mainly say that because our property has a house on it that was actually moved out of the Okefenokee swamp. When the wildlife refuge, the national government, I guess, actually took over the swamp, [they] made it a refuge and would not allow the people who already lived in the swamp to hunt and trap anymore," she told Bowen.

One of the sons of W.T. Chesser, who settled a small island on the eastern edge of the Okefenokee Swamp in the late 1850s, now known as Chesser Island, moved his house out of the swamp and onto the property she and her husband currently own, she said, and the house she currently lives in was built by W.T. Chesser's great-grandson, Clifford, in 1959.

"This used to be inhabited by the Chesser family, and prior to that, Roddenberry, which is another big name around here," she explained. "So, we have some really old structures on our property. Like, you can still see the hand cut beams that they used to [chop] themselves to make everything. Our house, that we live in, is right next door to that old Chesser homestead that I spoke of."

According to the woman, they began experiencing paranormal events as soon as they moved in, beginning with an anomalous incident which may have involved her husband's cellphone.

We bought this property in 2016 and we were standing outside, me and my husband and my daughter's boyfriend at the time, were just standing around talking and the first thing that we experienced here [was] from my husband's body came his voice and the sound of him saying his dog's name with a whistle—the way he whistles for his dog—and then the dog bark. All three of us were just kind of looking around like "What the heck was that?"

And he went through his phone, there's nothing—no voice memos, no videos, no nothing—that does that. Well, it could have been his phone, which was in his pocket. We just know that it came from his body, like his legs. It probably was from his phone. We've had quite a few things that have happened from our phones in here.

"So, that was the first thing," she added. "You know, we didn't think too much of it other than 'Wow, that was weird.'"

But the family continued to have strange experiences on the property, including those members who were just visiting.

> My sister was here sleeping in the living room, and she has sleep apnea. She's from Canton, you probably know where Canton [is]. She has sleep apnea, but we have dogs in the house, so because of the dog hair she didn't bring her CPAP machine.
>
> So, she was sleeping on the recliner in our living room, and she woke up to what she thought at first was my husband picking on her, telling her "Boo," right when he woke up in the middle of the night or, you know, he'd leave for work early in the morning or something.
>
> Well, when she woke up and thought she heard "boo," she felt a puff of air in her face and then she says "I don't think they said boo, I think they said breathe." Because she was having one of those [episodes] people get with sleep apnea where they stop breathing. She felt a puff of air in her face, and something said "breathe." That was kind of neat.

At least two other incidents involving sleeping persons interacting with unknown forces occurred in the house, she recalled.

The first, she said. involved her daughter's boyfriend.

"My daughter's boyfriend was here in the same living room, he was asleep, and she came and was trying to wake him up. It was later in the morning, so it was time for him to be up anyway," she said. "He described this as, he said like sleep paralysis, but something would not let him wake up, and he could see my daughter at like the end of a hallway. He was trying to get to her, trying to come up, trying to wake up, [but he] couldn't wake up."

The second involved the woman's mother.

> Along those same lines, my mother was staying with us, staying in my daughter's bedroom, and had a similar incident to that. I was up working, I work from home. I was up early one morning, and I kept hearing these weird, weird, strange noises. Well, my mother kind of kicked my daughter out of her bedroom and she slept in the living room while my mom was in her bedroom, and these noises, I could kind of think, "Well, maybe that's my daughter waking up,"

because sometimes, my teenage girls, they wake up and [they'll call for me].

You know, they're just moaning because they woke up and they want me to get them something to drink or something like that. I kept hearing this noise, and this was five or six something in the morning, way too early for her to be awake.

And the dog, her dog, was actually sitting there with me, too, and she started getting real curious as to the noise. I finally, after this went on for 10 minutes, I'm like "Oh my gosh, what is this noise."

And I'm going to describe the noise, please don't laugh at me, it was like [makes breathy screeching sound]. So, then I started getting creeped out by it.

I walked out of my office, and I went first towards my daughter to see if it was her, and she was still sound asleep. I didn't have to get too far, because I heard the noise coming from my daughter's bedroom, which is where my mother is sleeping. So, I get close to the door, and it's closed, and I kind of put my ear up to the door and I hear the noise continue.

I knocked on the door slightly, like "Mom?"

Well then, because we had other incidents of stuff happen in the house, I was scared, like "Am I going to open up this door and see my mom flying around the ceiling or something?"

I was just like, "Do I open the door? Of course, I have to, that's my mom. I have to go check on my mom."

I opened the door, and she's lying just flat, middle of the bed, no movement whatsoever, but I continued to hear the noise. So, I walked towards her, the noise is coming from her mouth. But she's just as still as could be. I checked to make sure that she was okay. I put my hand on her leg and kind of gave her a little shake, and I said, "Mom, are you okay?" And she still didn't move, didn't respond, but the noise stopped.

I couldn't wait for my daughter to wake up so I could tell her what happened. 10 minutes after I told her that, so let's say three hours later, probably, my mother comes out of the bedroom. And normally, she's 77 years old, she normally would go straight to the restroom. She came out of the bedroom, and she said, "Let me tell you what happened to me last night."

She said, "Something had its hands on my shoulders, holding me down, and I was screaming help. I was screaming 'help, help.' And you never came."

So, that kind of creeped me out. I was like, "Whoa."

She said something, she described it as a man, a black figure, a man, was holding her down.

If she has ever had [sleep paralysis], she has never mentioned it.

Another incident experienced by the woman involved her cellphone, similar to the previous story involving her husband.

"So, one evening I had my phone, which at the time wasn't an old phone. I had it in my kitchen, plugged in. My husband was watching TV and I had left the living room to go use the restroom. Often times, he'll watch YouTube videos while he's waiting on me. I was hearing a lot of racket, a lot of noise, and I wondered what the heck he was watching. When I got up to go back into the living room, I had to stop and head towards my phone because my phone, which was in the kitchen, was just making this godawful, bloodcurdling scream noise, like a woman screaming," she said. "I grabbed my phone, took it to my husband, and said 'Oh my gosh, listen to my phone.' I started frantically closing every app that was open. I showed him that there was nothing open on my phone, and I'm still getting this scream, like a bloodcurdling scream coming from my phone."

"When I say bloodcurdling scream, I am not joking," she added. "It was like a woman screaming in agony. So, that was pretty creepy."

Her most recent experience, she said, involved hearing footsteps approaching her during remodeling of the house.

Most recently, it was later in the evening. We'd been going through some remodeling in the house, and everything had been quiet for over a year, we had not heard anything since we started the remodel. I was standing in our bedroom looking down our new hallway, we didn't even have a hallway before, but I was looking down the new hallway trying to decide which rug I was going to put in this area.

We had one portion of our house, which was the living room, closed off with a piece of plastic to keep the dust to a minimum when they were sanding the walls and such, and while the contractor was not here, we pulled the plastic back a little bit, so, you know, we weren't blocked off from our living room and kitchen, and could reach the back of our house. I was standing there, again, thinking about what rug I was going to put in this area, and I hear a disturbance in the living room.

My husband and our dogs were all asleep, but I figured, you know, the dogs were moving around. Well, then I heard the crumble of that plastic, like you're walking through the plastic, and then I saw it move. Then I heard a few footsteps come down the hallway, across from the plastic, towards me.

Of course, then, I'm just frozen, freaked out. I got really, really cold, and then in my new bathroom, which used to be my office, the shower turned on. It wasn't full on, and it wasn't just a drip, [nor was it] like it was dripping after somebody took a shower. It was like a slow water flow, I guess you could say. That lasted 20 seconds and I took off and hid in my bed. Which was in the living room at the time, because our whole house was torn apart.

Me and my husband were by ourselves, both of our girls are grown and married. It was just he and I there. He had been asleep for several hours and our dogs were in there with him. I did peek in the shower, I looked in the shower in my bathroom to see if I saw anything, but I didn't. I just took off running.

On previous occasions, she said, her daughter had been "sitting on the bathtub, shaving her legs on the side of the bathtub, and the cold water turned on. The faucet just straight up turned on," and they'd both heard footsteps "walking across the hard wood floors not even 20 feet away from us."

One of the contractors also reportedly experienced the phenomenon.

"My contractor was here and one day he heard—and this was in the middle of the day, which was unusual—footsteps in the house," she said. "He thought that I was home. I wasn't home, and all the dogs were outside. He messaged me to ask me if my husband was coming home early, because he didn't want to come back inside."

Shadowy beings have also been reported in the living room.

"My daughter saw an apparition [of a shadow person]," the woman said. "Both my daughter and her new husband have seen them, and on separate occasions. In my living room, both of them were in my living room."

The phenomena occur outside the house, too, she said.

"Outside, my husband, he has a [detached] garage, and of course a lot of power equipment out there," she said. "My husband has had power equipment turn on. His sander, a hand palm sander. He's a very cautious, safety-oriented guy. He's a lineman, so if he's not safe, he dies, or somebody dies. So, he says that a sander that he had on the counter turned on and vibrated off the counter out in his shop. He says that he has also seen an image of an old man in overalls, leaned over and looking at his tractor."

Even her husband's father has experienced strange events on their property.

"My father-in-law, who's a retired detective and police officer, he brings his RV down here, and on two separate occasions he's had a knock on his door," she said. "One time the door opened up. You literally have to pull the thing and latch it. The door just opened right up, and nothing was there."

The woman said an empath, her "daughter's best friend's mother," visited the property and told her that "she feels when she goes outside, not far away from our house but still on our property, she says there are just men. There are just men working right there, non-stop working. They don't know to stop. They're all over. She says they're just working, working, working."

Trader's Hill, only a few miles away, did have a considerable lumber business, and an old railway does run along their property.

According to the empath, "a little boy got trampled by a horse" when the property "was just farmland," and his mother later hanged herself.

I wasn't able to verify these deaths, although it's worth noting that Charlton County did not keep official death records before 1919.

The empath also claimed that suspicious dirt found in the couple's bedroom was from "the little boy playing in the garden. She said that he's showing us what he's doing in the garden. She said that his presence and the mother's presence is very, very strong in here."

"It was constant," the woman said of the dirt. "I would sweep it up and then I would get dirt again. You know, not every night, but frequently. We take our shoes off at the door. We never walk through the house with our shoes on, because we have chickens and pigs and you know, we got dirty feet."

Ultimately, these events are something the family has learned to live with.

"It gives me the heebie-jeebies and it scares me, but it's nothing bad that's happened to me or my husband," said the woman.

Less than 10 miles southwest of this woman's house is the Suwanee Canal Recreation Area, wherein a rather bizarre disturbance occurred just over two decades ago.

Interestingly enough, The Singular Fortean Society received the report describing the anomaly in the same month as Aubrey spoke to the witness who shared her account of the haunted assisted living home.

The time dilation described by the woman in that case reminded me of this one, which came from Shirley Ivey; a woman who said she, her husband, their teenage daughters, and at least two strangers all experienced a strange spacetime distortion while visiting the Okefenokee Swamp in Georgia.

According to Shirley, the unusual event took place on Monday, April 3rd, 2000, when she was 41 years old.

This happened in the Okefenokee Swamp in southeast Georgia. On our way to Florida from our home in Michigan at the time, we stopped at the Suwanee Canal Recreation Area. While there we decided to rent a motorboat and go up the canal to a picnic area for lunch. The waterway is on a meandering canal.

Conditions were "low and trashy" so there was no chance of getting lost on any of the small tributaries because there was no way of getting through. The canal was fairly wide and easy to follow. We enjoyed the dark and mysterious water and the moss draped cypress of this ancient swamp. But then we noticed that it seemed to be taking a very long time to go the few miles or so to the picnic area.

We finally made it and walked on the "trembling earth" to the picnic area. I definitely made sure to note which way to go upon leaving the picnic spot. After lunch, as we were preparing to push off, two young men approached us in another motorboat. They were in a distressed state and asked if they could follow us back to the concession. They said they could not get through. We agreed to allow them to follow us. I had observed that they did not appear to be drunk.

After about 30 feet, we came to a stop because our way was

blocked by a strip of dry land with tall grass growing on top. I could see the canal continuing beyond the barrier. We considered portaging over it but concluded it was not a good idea in a wild swamp. I even touched the side of the bank, and it was solid. We looked back at the two guys, and they shrugged their shoulders.

We could do only one thing and that was to go back to the picnic area to see if we could possibly have veered off course. We had not.

On the way back we passed an elderly couple paddling a canoe in the direction of the barrier (unusual because we had not encountered anyone else in a canoe). I tried to warn them about the blockage ahead, but they only kept their focus ahead with no acknowledgement, as if we were not even there.

When we reached the picnic area, we decided to try again. This time we not only had no barriers in the way, but we seemed to have gotten there very quickly.

Those two guys got out of their boat and peeled rubber in the parking lot before I could even discuss this event with them. The people at the concession were no help as far as information on others experiencing similar problems.

In further correspondence with me, Shirley clarified that their experience took place "between mile marker 3 and 4 at the Suwannee Canal Recreation Area."

"The blockage had a bank about 18 inches high and dry with tall grass," she said. "I now live along Cross Creek in Florida, and I know it was not a tussock. Although there were no strange sounds, lights, or fog, time seemed to be warped."

In a swamp, tussocks refer to drifting masses of herbaceous plants. They can range in size from a few feet across to hundreds of acres. Floating islands, a phenomenon similar to tussocks, are formed from peat, mud, and plants, and can sometimes support trees of up to 50 feet tall and 12 inches in diameter.

"The concessionaire had mentioned an old Indian burial ground in the area," added Shirley.

Okefenokee Swamp—at nearly 700 square miles—is North America's largest blackwater swamp, and was once home to a thriving indigenous population, including peoples of the Deptford, Swift Creek, and Weeden Island cultures. Archeological evidence shows that the in-

TOP: A photo taken during Shirley's trip to Okefenokee Swamp in Georgia

LEFT: Shirley and family during their trip to the swamp.

PHOTO CREDIT: Shirley Ivey

digenous peoples lived in the area as early as 2500 BC, and numerous mounds have been found in and around the swamp. Okefenokee Swamp served as the border for the Mocoma, Timucua, and Apalachee nations, who occupied the area until they were forced out by European settlers in the late 18th and early 19th centuries. The Mocama and Timucua nations were members of the Creek Confederacy and thought to be descendants of the area's early Mound Builders. The last indigenous population to occupy the swamp were people of the Seminole Nation, who used Okefenokee as cover from the United States government until the U.S. Army chased them out in 1838.

Some of the mounds built by the area's original inhabitants were used for the burial of prominent persons within their communities, although it is unclear how that would relate to the perceived spacetime distortion had by Ivey and company. American Indian mounds and other burial sites are often associated with increased incidents of paranormal activity by European settlers and their descendants, although there is no evidence to support any stronger correlation between those sites and the paranormal than there is between such phenomena and European cemeteries.

However, incidents of high strangeness are reported in and around bodies of water quite frequently, such as the unexplained, haunting melody heard by Angela Nichols and her family one afternoon during the summer of 1987 while fishing on the Saline River in Arkansas.

Angela reached out to The Singular Fortean Society in December of 2019 to tell us about the mysterious song.

According to her initial report,

It was [1987] … I was just a girl. My mom and dad took my sister and I up stream in a flat bottom fishing boat on the Saline River in south central Arkansas.

The idea was to motor up where people didn't go and tie off in the middle to fish. We went a mile or more from the camp and tied off where a tree was laid over the river.

As soon as a hook was dropped in the water the boat began vibrating. Not harshly, just subtly, and we could hear song. By song...I don't know how to explain. There were no words, and it was the most beautiful sound I ever heard in my life. The boat vibrated with the melody. Three of us thought it must be coming from under the water.

My dad was not so sure. He pulled over to the east bank and got out looking around the woods. Then we went to the west bank. He climbed up the embankment to see an open field, but he never found anything to explain it.

The longer we were there the more profound the vibrations became...again it was the most beautiful sound I have ever heard. We may have been there 10 to 15 minutes. Just long enough for Dad to be afraid of the unknown, not finding [an] explanation...we never went back.

I have never experienced anything else like it. Never heard anyone else describe anything like it. It may always remain a mystery what happened, and it was so long ago.

I just happened across one of your stories and decided to share.

I followed up with Angela, who added more details through a series of emails.

She described the sound as "steady flowing with melody. No breaks in the sound or the boat vibrations, but it did get stronger/louder the longer we were there."

"It was higher notes. Maybe mid to high. No low notes. No distinct sounds...flowing like a song. no pauses just awesome and scary and intriguing. If there was a way to know I would choose to know," said Angela.

"I have never heard anything else like it," she added. "Most beautiful thing I have ever heard. Not like scary music in a movie. The sound alone was not threatening in any way, it was not a sound someone would want to run from, but rather that you could listen to forever."

Whatever its origin, the sound made a strong impression on her and her family.

"Everyone that was in the boat that day are still living and all of us remember," she said. "It's not a forgettable thing to encounter."

"We were in a very remote location," Angela continued. "A gravel road that trailed off in places. It's gated now and you have to be a member of a hunting lease to get the key. Back then only a few people knew of the river access point. Most of them didn't even bring in boats because the fishing was so good from the bank. Many nights extended family camped there and we would go visit during the day. I was [seven years old] at the time. That may be young, but I remember plenty from back then."

"My sister and I used to talk about it growing up. It's not easy to leave something alone that you want to understand," she added.

Angela explained that she and her sister considered mermaids and sirens as possible explanations, but now she entertains the idea that "maybe it was something new, and by that I meant something that had not been encountered or at least recorded in history."

She added that her mother thought that it must have been an angel, since the sound was so beautiful.

"Our parents told us we shouldn't talk about it because people wouldn't believe it anyway, but we could talk about it as a family," she said. "Anyway, when I think of it, even though it was beautiful...I think it must have been a warning. It didn't start until we dropped a hook in the water. In the recesses of my mind, I think of a mother protecting her babies. Trying to scare off danger."

The sound described by Angela—especially given the effect it had on her—reminded me of nothing so much as faerie music. For centuries, people have reported hearing enchanting melodies in lonely places that they later struggle to describe or remember. Legend has it that if a person must travel out alone at night, then they should beware any strange lights or music, because to become distracted by such supernatural stimuli could lead to a most dreadful interaction with the faerie folk. Stories exist that tell of people being struck blind for interrupting faeries dancing in their ring, or even literally dancing themselves to death.

A few years ago, I had a wonderful conversation with Sheila, who played with The Currach Irish Trio, about faerie music.

"Passionate musicians sometimes hear something that drives them crazy," she said to me. "And afterwards they try frantically to remember."

Sheila told me about a song called Paddy's Rambles through the Park. According to legend, there was once a man walking home late at night, and as he passed a graveyard, he heard music of a most enthralling nature. The man was immediately obsessed and followed the song into the cemetery.

The man memorized the melody and wrote it down as soon as he was able.

It's a popular song, and one that's freely available online. Sheila described it as "haunting, spooky, and unusual."

In another version of the story I found, the man stumbles through a faerie fort, as opposed to a graveyard, but is enchanted by the music all the same.

Another song she spoke of is called the Faerie Reel. This piece of otherworldly composition is both a song and a dance that are commonly found together. The origin of this one is a little murkier, but it involves a man who encountered a strange gentleman one night.

"Out of the shadows comes a guy that says, 'I'm going to play a tune you'll never forget,'" said Sheila of the song.

The man frantically tried to remember it after the fact, and the Faerie Reel was built out of that.

Sheila described that tune as having an "enchanting quality."

"It sets my hair on edge," she laughed. "When I first heard it, I said, 'That's a faerie tune, of course it is.'"

Faerie music is said to have the ability to beguile the hearts of men, and if you're not careful you can lose an entire night to it, or in some cases even years. Luckily, no such fate befell Angela or her family; the only time they lost was what they've spent thinking about it since.

Much of the lore surrounding faeries overlaps with other areas of the paranormal, including UFOs, abduction phenomena, and hauntings; I can only guess what the sound's true origin might be. All I can say is what it reminded me of, and that's the haunting, elusive melodies of the Fair Folk.

An equally compelling mystery is the case presented to me by a woman who wished to share a number of anomalous events she'd experienced in northern Idaho while living in a cabin near the foot of Mica Mountain.

"I lived up there for eight years, in a cabin with no running water," she said. "I had a very modern job, but my life was very simple away from work. I loved it out there."

"When I moved out there, I had a lot of issues. I had a lot of experiences that I would not have thought would happen before," she continued. "But whenever they'd happen to me there, I always tried to make them normal. Instead of wild flights of fancy, you see crazy things and you try to say 'Oh, this is something that I know about.'"

The first such incident recounted involved a phantom bonfire seen from her property in the fall of 2007.

"I had a bit of a commute, and by the time I got home it was starting to get dark," she explained. "I had a loop that I liked to ride through the woods that had some nice jumps, and then I'd come up over a hill and I could look at my home, and down at this cabin. So, I was up at the top of the hill, and I saw a fire burning down there—it was a big fire—not an out-of-control fire, but a bonfire. I heard chanting."

Although she had been to the cabin before in the daylight, she did not know the people who owned it well; they lived in town and rarely used the cabin.

Despite that, she thought the owners might have been responsible for the incident—at least until she visited the cabin to see for herself.

"It wasn't people sitting around the fire talking, it really did sound like Native American chanting. But still, I told myself, you know, it's the people who live there. I sat there for a while, and I listened, and then I headed home. I was like a quarter mile from home at that point. It was maybe a day or two later when I had a chance—I rode over there in daylight. And there was no fire pit, there was no burned ground, there was nothing," she said.

The witness never got the chance to ask her neighbors about it.

"I didn't know them very well," she said. "I couldn't really ask them."

The next incident she related was a sighting of strange lights over nearby Mica Mountain in the winter of 2009. She was approximately an eighth of a mile away from her previous sighting.

"We lived in a kind of a snowy area—we'd get four feet of snow. In fact, sometimes I'd have to shovel my windows we had so much snow...A snowy night can just be incredibly beautiful when the stars are out, and I was about ready to go to bed but I didn't quite want to go to bed yet; so I went out and I had just fed the horses, and I leaned my arms over the horse's back, you know, they're warm and fuzzy and just a nice thing to stand next to in the cold, and I looked up at the mountain," she said. "I looked at the top of the mountain and saw these lights."

At first, she thought they might be the headlights of several vehicles driving on top of the mountain, but she quickly realized that wasn't the case—the lights were above the mountain, and there was no cloud cover off which any lights from the ground could reflect.

"I tried to tell myself 'Well, maybe somebody's driving around up there.' Except these lights, they were above the mountain. They were not touching the mountain," she said.

There were, I don't know, seven or eight of them. Quite a few. And they were just balls of white light. That's what it looked like from where I was. I watched them and I thought "How would I describe what I'm seeing?" They looked like they were playing. They would leapfrog over the top of each other. They would shoot off at just incredible speeds. And then they would just stop. Just like in an instant.

As if that wasn't enough, I thought, "I've got to figure out what these are. I just have to know." I jumped in my truck in my pajamas and a coat and headed for the mountain. The mountain was snowed in at that point, but I got as close to it on county roads as I could get.

But the weird thing was, as soon as I went out my driveway, I couldn't see them anymore, even though I still had a clear view of the mountain. And I headed east, and then north towards the mountain, and took the county road and headed back west and just made a loop and came back. And as soon as I drove back down my driveway, I could see them again. I thought, 'This is too weird.' I watched them for a little while, and then it kind of weirded me out that they disappeared when I got off of my property, and I went to bed.

The lights, she said, were "many times bigger than a star. Relative to the mountain, and this may not be very accurate, but my best guess is that they were like the size of a tree on the mountain, so, 20 feet? They were big."

The sighting was impactful enough to her that she was certain it must have made the news, but the next day nobody else seemed to have seen it.

"I really, sincerely thought it would be on the news. And there was nothing. Probably, I was the only one who saw it or could see it," she said.

The final sighting from the property that she shared was of an unknown hairy hominid. This sighting took place in the summer of 2010.

"I was out on my property in the daylight during summertime, and I saw something crossing the pasture just to the east of us. I thought, 'that's a calf moose, that's a young moose,' because it was so awkward looking, and it was about the size of a yearling moose," she said.

But she quickly realized that what she was looking at was no moose.

"It was walking on two legs and [was] definitely not a moose," she said. "It was much larger [in both height and weight] than a human and moved in a slightly hunched over way. Other than that, it had a dark coat; I can't say much about the length of the coat [because I was too far away]. There was both an awkwardness and a power about it."

She was struck both by how quickly the creature noticed her and how it seemed to so suddenly disappear.

"And as soon as I saw it, it looked right at me," she said. "It was like a quarter of a mile away, and I wasn't making any noise. It was too fast, it just noticed me too fast. It felt psychic. Once again, I became kind of obsessed, and I chased after it. I'm not a fast runner, but I ran as hard as I could...it went through a small bunch of cows in a small pasture that's not used much, and it just wasn't there. I thought 'It must have moved very quickly and very silently, so it didn't disturb the cows. How did it get away so quick?' Before that moment I would have said, Bigfoot is probably not true. But then I read about it and the thing that most resonated with me was Bigfoot as an interdimensional being. Because of the way it was so quickly aware of that I had seen it. And how, almost magically, it had seemed to disappear."

I couldn't help but ask her if she was familiar with the idea of sighting "window areas," and if she thought that her cabin might have been in one.

"That's a new angle. I hadn't thought of that before," she said. "That mountain, it's just full of mica. In some of my reading about ghost lights, they do mention ley lines and mica. And so, I always thought that maybe it's the mountain."

This wasn't the first time someone has mentioned ley lines to me—paths drawn between landmarks that some believe represent a natural energy unrecognized by modern science—but it's difficult to know what to do with that information. It felt like trying to explain one mystery with another, something I am generally loath to do. I'm perfectly happy to speculate in the name of exploration or put a common label on phenomena that share certain qualities, but I draw the line at circular reasoning.

Whatever the case may be, living in the area certainly seemed to have an effect on the woman. She mentioned that a year after her sighting of the lights over Mica Mountain, she had seen something similar in the springtime while visiting her brother.

"I was at my brother's house, 400 miles from there, and I was out in his horse pasture talking to his horses, and this thing flew overhead," she said. "It's near an air force base—Mountain Home Air Force Base— and I thought, 'Oh, this must be a bunch of jets in formation.' But relative to one another, they weren't moving at all. So, I thought this must be solid. If it's solid, it's not that far off the ground, maybe three telephone poles—100 to 200 feet up at the most—completely soundless, and it was in a 'V' formation."

"I have no clue what I saw," she added. "I can only speculate."

"The question that brings up to me, I was living on that property at the time I visited my brother and saw the unidentified object. Was that the land influencing me?" she asked. "Prior to living there, I had never heard of or seen or believed in any of this stuff. Since I've left, I've never seen anything unexplained again."

While the things experienced by her while living at the cabin may have left her with more questions than answers, she at least felt that the experiences were overall positive.

"I loved it out there, and weird things happened, and I never felt unsafe," she said. "But they certainly changed my worldview."

Maybe that was the point. Whatever these phenomena represent, that they have an often profound effect on those who witness them is undeniable.

In February of 2019, a man emailed us at The Singular Fortean Society to recount how he and a friend had reportedly seen a "shadowy man" transform into "a big, black shadowy cat-like creature" after suddenly appearing out of a "flash of bright light." An event not unlike the one experienced by my friend who had been healed during her nighttime visitation, although somewhat darker in its execution.

The following sounds crazy, but I promise it happened exactly as described. My wonder is if anyone has ever reported something similar. Years ago, a friend, myself, and my collie were sitting in my driveway at around 11 p.m. just BSing on a summer night.

Suddenly my dog began to go crazy and beg to go inside. Then, across the street, there was a quick flash of bright light and a shadowy man stepped out of the light. The man turned to look at us, and as he/it did, it went down on all fours and went from a shadowy man to a big, black, shadowy, cat-like creature. There was another flash of light, and it was gone.

During the event neither one of us spoke, but afterwards I looked at [my friend] and said, "do you want to go inside?"

He said "yes," and so we did.

Inside we took turns describing the event to each other and both of us saw the exact same thing. Years later I ran into this friend again and he still remembers every detail exactly the same. No drugs or alcohol were involved nor had either of us tried any of that yet. It was clear as day and I remember every detail like it was yesterday. I know we saw something; I am wondering if anyone knows what it was.

After that initial contact with the man, subsequent communication was done via email due to his schedule.

He described to me a profound feeling of "nothingness" prior to the experience.

"It was very still, like described before a tornado hits," he said. "The only one affected prior to it appearing was my collie, Rocky. He went batshit nuts running from us to the side door, begging to go inside. Rocky was older and never acted that way. He would sometimes stay out all day or night just doing his thing. After it happened and we went in, that dog laid next to us or at our feet and never budged."

"A light breeze was blowing but had stopped prior to [the event]," he added. "No crickets, cicadas, when I say nothing, I mean NOTHING. It was as if everything else knew something was up."

According to the man, this sighting took place in Richmond, Indiana, at around 11 p.m., in either the 3rd or 4th week of June 1993; he was not sure of the exact day.

Richmond is about 35 miles southeast of the Prairie Creek Reservoir, the site of a series of reports involving flying humanoids and glowing orbs—part of the Lake Michigan Mothman investigation. Indiana had seen a recent spate of such reports around the time this man reached out to discuss his experience, not only near the reservoir, but also surrounding the city of Gary. Strange activity reported out of Gary, a city of over 75,000 that sits on the shore of Lake Michigan, included sightings of both flying humanoids and gigantic pterodactyls.

"As for other strange occurrences in [our immediate] area, we had typical small, Midwestern town stories," the man said. "My friends and I used to go and look for supernatural occurrences. We had quite a few, but it was high school, and most could probably be chalked up to group hysterics."

The same can't be said for Indiana resident Garry Patterson, who certainly wasn't suffering from group hysterics during the many incidents in which he witnessed strange balls of light around the Prairie Creek Reservoir.

"I'm about seven miles from [the Prairie Creek Reservoir]," Garry told me. "I've seen many balls of light in this area, from Farmland towards Muncie."

"They are intelligent," he continued. "I've seen them react… change color, move, or shut off."

The now 53-year-old man stated that his family moved to the area in 1979, and his first sighting of a glowing orb in the area was in the summer of 1981, when he was 12.

"It was a clear summer night sky," Garry said. "I saw an orange/amber colored ball of light about 20 feet above the trees. It started towards me slowly, so I ran in and got my mom, when we came back out it was over our trees. The actual size is hard to say but I'd guess three feet across. It was totally silent, and it moved off to the west out of sight behind the trees."

"Funny thing, probably the summer before, I used to blink one of those old flashlights with the switch and button into the sky," he added.

Since his initial sighting in '81, Garry said he's had many sightings of strange glowing orbs in the area.

"I'm guessing I've seen them eight or so times where they were either red or orange, and maybe three to four where they were white," he said. "The [second to last] time was a few years back [in the summer of 2016]. I was driving east coming home at night, when I spotted an orb that was orange, and it seemed like a second one right next to it was changing back and forth from red to orange and dimming to dark and back. So, I got to my road turning south and I came to a stop to watch. The car window was down, so I fumbled with my phone to hit record… snap, gone."

Garry's most recent sighting came on Friday, May 29th, 2020. He contacted me just after arriving home to tell me he'd seen three amber-colored orbs south of Muncie, Indiana.

"I was driving east just south of Muncie, Indiana at approximately [12:40 am] when I saw [an orb] straight [to my] east. Then, when I could see better, there was another [orb] more to the south," he said.

Garry described the orbs as amber in color and said there was no movement or flashing. They appeared coin-sized, but he couldn't discern what their actual size was.

"It's really hard to tell with a light, but most have appeared the same size, and are usually the same color: amber/orange," he said. "I do know the one to the north looked bigger; it was a steeper angle, more above me. To be close enough or large enough for one to look larger above me, I would guesstimate three to four feet across, no smaller."

As he watched, "the one straight to the east 'shut off,' so I looked around and there was one that seemed closer to the north."

"As I was driving, there were trees in the way on some parts," he continued. "Then the one to the north 'shut off.' I could still see the one to the southeast, then it was gone also."

Garry couldn't find any mundane explanation for the orbs.

"I saw no airplanes and it was cloudy to the east, with broken cloud cover overhead," he said.

Historical weather data confirmed that the sky was mostly cloudy at the time of Garry's sighting.

The area south of Muncie is rural and no obvious landmarks or easily identified phenomena would seem to explain Patterson's sighting, given his description of events.

Garry's sightings have occurred in the area south of and between Muncie, Parker City, and Farmland, near Windsor, and align themselves with a 2,000-year-old Native American burial plot in the shape of an oval that covers an acre of land. To the west of the sightings and the mound, in a nearly straight line, lie the Prairie Creek Reservoir and Mounds State Park.

The line formed by these sightings and the associated landmarks is less than 200 miles north of the 37th Parallel, known as the United States' 'UFO Highway.' Stretching from Santa Cruz, California to the Chesapeake Bay, this area is known for UFO sightings, cattle mutilations, and other anomalous phenomena.

Some researchers suspect the 37th Parallel to run along a powerful ley line—those mysterious paths drawn between landmarks that are reputedly composed of earth energies—although we can't know for sure.

"I know things are found along ley lines," Garry said. "Since the

Mothman sighting at Prairie Creek, that makes a rough line from there to here and also Mounds State Park."

As far as what he believes the orbs might be, Garry, who identifies as a Christian, could say only that he does not believe they are any technology known to man.

"I know what the various things at night look like," he said. "As to what I think is behind the orbs...I believe they are a part of the spiritual or supernatural realm. [They] do things aircraft or pilots could never do."

He might be right. Given the descriptions of these phenomena provided to us by witnesses, it's difficult to maintain the belief that they have any basis in materialist science. That's especially true for the winged humanoids seen around the reservoir.

In February of 2019, just before Garry first contacted me about those mysterious glowing orbs, Lon received a report from a witness who claimed to have seen a flying humanoid with "glowing yellowish eyes" while on a boat at the Prairie Creek Reservoir in 2007. I was able to personally verify the identity of this witness but will not disclose further information for privacy reasons.

I am originally from Muncie, Indiana, and grew up spending a lot of time at Prairie Creek because my family has a boat there.

It was summer 2007 when we had taken a boat ride and watched the sunset. It was dusk and the sun was setting as we approached our dock. As we got closer my friend and I both saw what looked like a human standing at the end of our dock and thought it was strange because there was no one else around —our neighboring boats were all docked, there were no other cars around, etc. We were the only one out that evening from our dock area.

It then turned around and we saw its glowing yellowish eyes. At this point, we were freaked out wondering what this was because there was something totally off about it and it was clearly not a normal human. Then, as we got even closer, it spread its wings, flapped a few times and soared up into the sky. It was WAY too big to be a bird...I've never seen anything like it before or after. It was probably around five to six feet tall and really dark, the whole body and wings were gray/black.

Not sure if this is of interest but my family and I also saw a UFO at Prairie Creek Reservoir around dusk, as well, a few years later. We were one of the only boats on the water, it was such a serene, quiet and peaceful evening. My mother looked up at the sky and saw the UFO, so we all looked up, it was shaped like a tin can, stayed still, and made absolutely no noise. At that instant, my father caught a fish and the commotion caused us all to look down and a few seconds later when we looked back up it was gone without a trace.

"The eyewitness is a known credible media professional," said Lon of the person from whom he received the account.

Their career was the main impetus behind taking such care to guard their identity. Like I've said before, witnesses really run the gamut in terms of career and socioeconomic status, and some of them really have lot to lose by having their name attached to this kind of story. We're working hard to erode the societal stigma surrounding these sightings, but at this point, I don't blame people who choose to remain anonymous.

The eye color described by this witness is very similar to that reportedly seen in the same area by another witness in the winter of 2011—in that case, the creature's eyes were said to be "greenish yellowish-like."

That sighting was reported by a woman who emailed Lon and said she was "driving down Road 1 in-between 400 and 500 S... in Randolph County just ten to fifteen minutes kind of east from Prairie Creek Reservoir."

As I was driving, I saw what appeared to be a human crouched down in the road. As I got closer, and the more I slowed down, it did not move, so I was at a complete stop. This thing slowly turned its head to look my way and it had greenish yellowish-like eyes, like the color of cat eyes.

It stared for maybe three seconds and then proceeded to slowly get up from its position, like a human would stand up because it had legs. It turned towards my car. It stepped on my car and used it to take off. Then it lifted off like a glider towards the sky.

I turned my head just in time to see it tuck its legs into its body, so it did appear as a bird in flight...kind of. Its wingspan was wider than anything I've ever seen on an animal in my life.

Her husband initially thought she'd encountered a bird of some kind, but later changed his mind after reviewing some of the other sighting reports.

As for the woman, she too chose to remain anonymous, and declined any further communication.

"I've never said anything to anyone else in fear that I would be made out to be an idiot," she said. "I also would still like to maintain my privacy as I do not want any public attention from this as I have a young daughter and do not want her to be bought into it either."

Like many before her, this woman was prompted to come forward after seeing another sighting report, this one from a man who said he'd seen a "bat-like" flying humanoid with "an obvious face" on December 26th, 2018, between 4 and 4:30 p.m.

Lon told me he'd spoken to this witness over the telephone.

"[The man] and his wife were traveling southbound on a county road, about a mile south of the Prairie Creek Reservoir near Muncie, Indiana," Lon said. "The date was December 26, 2018, at dusk. A huge flying object caught [his] attention."

[The witness] is a military veteran, hunter, trapper and farmer who lives in the immediate area," he continued. "His knowledge of military flying craft, wildlife and his keen sense of observance was apparent while I talked to him. The winged being that he was observing was unlike anything he had ever seen before. The creature was flying just above treetop level and was easily visible to the witness. His reaction was to slam on his brakes in wonderment, exclaiming to his wife 'do you see that?' His wife was shaken by the sudden stop and was unable to react fast enough to see the winged being."

The creature described by the witness was very similar to other reports of winged humanoids around Lake Michigan, including the stillness of its wings in flight.

"[He] stated that the being was humanoid in shape with an obvious 'face,'" Strickler said. "The body had a length of approximately six to seven feet, with bat-like wings that were extremely wide. The being was dark-colored and seemed to glide at a steady speed. He never noticed the flapping of wings while watching the creature."

According to the man, the creature's wings had a leathery texture. He was unable to discern if the creature had any additional limbs beyond its wings, nor could he recognize fine detail in its face.

Also similar to other sighting reports is the profound effect the experience had on this witness.

"[The man's] wife states that [he] has been truly affected by the incident and has constantly mentioned it to her, in an attempt to explain what this winged being really was," Lon said. "He had refused to mention the incident outside of his family. When [he] read about the recent sightings in Gary, Indiana, he called his wife from his job and asked her to contact me right away. He later called me when he got home. This witness was very forthcoming and anxious to find out what this creature was."

Those sightings in Gary included a husband and wife who, on separate occasions and individually of one another, had reportedly seen an enormous "prehistoric bird" in 2015 and 2016, and two witnesses who'd seen much smaller winged anomalies in 2018 and 2019, described as a flying creature with the body of a "large monkey" and wings "similar to bat wings", and a four-to-five-foot-tall "grayish" creature with "large wings…similar to bat wings," respectively.

As for the witness who desperately wanted answers to his questions regarding what he'd seen one winter's day in 2018, well, we didn't have any—nothing definitive anyway. The further I delve into these mysteries the less I seem to know, and I caution anyone who might be considering the journey to be wary of getting lost looking for answers in Mothman country.

CHAPTER 11

HUNTING THE HUNTERS

So far, we've seen unwitting victims and surprised observers, but not everyone is content to be accosted by monsters; sometimes, people arm themselves, and sometimes, they even start shooting.

In early April of 2020, just after the COVID-19 pandemic had shut down most of the country, The Singular Fortean Society received three videos from Colton Greenhaw, a resident of Rhinelander, Wisconsin, which featured eerie howls captured by Greenhaw and his friends and neighbors.

When I interviewed Colton a short time after receiving the videos, on April 4th, he told me that the videos had been recorded outside of his apartment the week prior.

"Kind of towards Highway 8, there's a little patch of woods by the edge of town and the apartment complex where we're at, and around nine or ten o'clock at night, every night, there's been some weird stuff going on out there," said Colton.

Colton said that he and his neighbors have all heard the sounds, and that he recorded two videos on his phone, while his neighbor recorded one on his GoPro camera.

"I got two videos on my phone," he said. "That was two nights ago. It's big, you can hear on the GoPro that it's big. We could hear it crashing as it walked through the woods. They're not small twigs breaking, they're pretty big sticks breaking. We haven't seen anything yet, but we put a deer cam out last night and we're putting another out on the other side of the forest tonight."

"We've been asking a lot of people, 'Have you heard anything weird?' We'll play the sound on our phone and they're like 'That's exactly what we heard,'" Colton added. "It's really loud at night, too, you could have your windows closed and you can hear it."

The apartment complex where Colton lives is situated across the Pelican River from the Holmboe Conifer Forest State Natural Area.

He told me that he'd seen evidence of something throwing rocks and disturbing waterfowl in the area, and that he and his friends had even found an unusual footprint.

"The crazy thing is, we [found the footprint] on our side of the shoreline, where the apartment is. The apartment is at the edge of the woods on the river, and then on the other side is national forest. But we got the footprint on our side. On our side is a little pond, and there's a bunch of ducks and geese, and then we've got a couple big rocks that are lying in the pathway and on the edge of the water, so I don't know if something is throwing them or whatever. They weren't there before. It could be a person throwing them on the path or kids playing, but the rocks are coming from the river and they're ending up on the walkway that people walk their dogs on and stuff," he explained. "Then at night, at about twelve o'clock at night, between twelve and three o'clock at night, something like that, you can hear the geese picking up and flying off, and I know they don't fly off at that time of night."

Colton added that the geese made considerable noise while flying off, honking as though something had frightened them.

According to him, a cast was made of the footprint.

"Everybody was watching us pull the cast out of the ground, and we're like 'What the hell is this,'" he said. "You can't see the toes very clearly, but you can see where they're at and it looks like there's four toes—when you put your hand in the print, you can feel the digits. There's only four of them."

"I don't [have a photo of the footprint cast] but I can get it, I think it's still sitting in my garage yet," he added. "That was three or four days ago now that they got that cast. It shocked the hell out of all of us. I mean, it's pretty obvious. At first, I thought it was a bear, we all did until the cast came out, but it's not a bear. It's pretty big. 14 inches long by 8 inches wide. You can tell where the toes are, but it only seems like there's four toes."

I requested photographs of the cast, but unfortunately never received any.

Waterfowl weren't the only wildlife disturbed by whatever was making the eerie howls, according to Colton.

"I mean, we have coyotes across the river and then they stopped and two days later this thing started to happen," he said. "Every night, you'd hear the coyotes take something down on the other side of the river, and it's loud, everybody hears them at night, but lately we haven't been hearing them at all."

The incidents in the spring of 2020 aren't the only unusual encounters that Colton and his friends have had around Rhinelander.

It's not our first encounter that we've had. My friends and I, we go have bonfires in the woods and stuff, way out in the middle of nowhere. You're driving three or four or five miles in the middle of nowhere and we saw something that was, well, none of us want to say what it is because we don't want to sound like idiots, but it looked pretty damn tall. I mean, it was huge, and it was at night—about twelve-thirty at night. I slammed on the brakes of my Toyota—this was out in the Parrish Trails— [my friend] grabbed his shotgun, and I grabbed my shotgun, and we're just sitting there while the thing watches us. And then it just slowly turns its head and it's gone. You can't hear anything crack or nothing, and it's just unbelievable how quiet whatever it is can be.

It was sitting right on the edge of the trail, and it looked like [where the creature was] the pine trees were sitting on a hill, but we walked in and they're actually in a hole and you could see that the eyes were right next to the trees. You could see it, it was something big. We thought it was something sitting in the trees, but it definitely wasn't something sitting in the trees because when it moved, it moved fast.

We stared at it for probably a minute to a minute and twenty seconds. We're all making eye contact with this thing and it's just scary as hell when it's just staring back at you. We locked the doors, grabbed our shotguns, and were like 'What the hell do we do? What is that?' It was weird.

We have bonfires out there all the time, and when it starts to mellow out, you can hear some weird stuff out in those woods. People freak out and end up leaving because they're afraid to camp out there.

The more recent howls appeared to ebb with a sudden influx of colder weather.

"My neighbor and I were talking last night while we let our dogs out, and it was snowing, and we were like 'I don't think we're going to hear anything,'" Colton explained. "It's starting to snow, and we had that cold front blow in the other night and both nights it's been dead quiet. But it was making all these noises when it was really warm out and nice out at night, with clear skies, but the second the clouds started to move in it just stopped."

Regardless of the reprieve brought by the weather, Colton insisted that people were on edge from the strange experiences.

"Nobody's walking at night anymore after hearing that stuff in Rhinelander," he said. "They're freaked out."

And as for himself, Colton wasn't sure what to make of the things he'd seen and heard.

"I don't know what to think of all this, to be honest with you. I don't know what to believe. Could be some redneck like myself out there doing something stupid to freak people out, but we're out on the edge of town and nobody in town is really doing anything out there. It all started happening when the coyotes went away, and then during this pandemic there's no action on the street—there's no cars running around or nothing at night—everybody's hunkered down, and that's when you hear it. It's probably close to the city, which is weird," he said. "All the neighbors now, we've all got pistols. We're being careful. We've all got guns now, and we're watching out, walking around with our guns at night. We're all scared."

Eerie howls similar to those captured by Colton and his neighbors had been recorded in Ohio in February 2020 and northern Ontario, Canada, in October 2019.

Skeptical explanations for the howls include everything from wolves to elk to moose to mountain lions or bobcats, although there are those who attribute the sounds to something more paranormal, like Bigfoot or even Dogman. Wolves and elk have seen a resurgence in northern Wisconsin within the last decade, and the occasional moose does wander down from Canada—but that doesn't explain Colton's sighting in the forest, or the continued activity reported by him and his friends.

On June 30th, 2020, we received the following email in response to an article about the eerie howls.

I wish to remain anonymous, but I wanted to report I've heard the same screams as the guy in the video. Weeks ago, I heard it in the middle of the night and ran in to check on my daughter. She was irritated that I woke her up but was [otherwise] fine. I passed it off as a dream, maybe.

Anyhow, I was not sleeping and heard it again last night. It was shrilling and sounded like it was right outside my window. My dogs were too scared to leave the porch and refused to go out. I don't know what it is, but for sure it's running around close to Lake Tomahawk.

Lake Tomahawk is a town of just over 1,100 people—nestled within Wisconsin's 1.5 million acre Chequamegon-Nicolet National Forest—and is about 20 miles northwest of Rhinelander.

Based on when the email was sent, the first set of "screams" described by this witness could have taken place around the same time as those reported by Colton and the second set could have been as recent as June 29th.

I responded to the email, saying that The Singular Fortean Society is happy to respect the privacy of anyone who contacts them and asking the witness to please contact me with any developments.

So far, there has been no further correspondence.

Luckily, despite Colton and his friends and neighbors being armed, nobody fired a shot, at least none of which I was aware. The same can't be said of a woman with whom Aubrey spoke in December of 2020.

Georgia resident Alana Strickland told Aubrey that she and her friends shot at an anomalous humanoid while camping off of the Appalachian Trail on Georgia's Blood Mountain one warm June night in 2012 at around 11 p.m.

I was out camping with some friends in Blood Mountain, which is up in the north part of Georgia along the Appalachian Trail. I was 20 [years old] at the time, and I will go on record and say that I was not drinking. We had a bonfire, and we were pretty mellow. We weren't whooping and hollering, we were mostly hanging around telling stories from the week and whatnot. We heard something over on what would have been my right side, towards the denser part of the woods. We were only about five miles off of the main trail, so we weren't terribly far. It had only taken us about a day to get there.

We heard something pretty big. Most of us were hunters that were there, so we could pretty much distinguish between squirrels, bear, [and] deer—so, we heard something really big, and we assumed [it was a] bear. Like any good, red-blooded Americans, we got our guns, and just to make sure, because you don't shoot unless you can see it, we got our lights and we walked out there to see what it was. A lot of the girls were making high-pitched squeaking noises because [they were frightened], versus me and the guys who went out there and thought it was probably nothing and we'd scare it off.

Right in the tree line, our lights kept catching something big and reflective that was probably about six feet or so tall. If it was standing just behind the trees, its eyes were about six feet above the ground. Which is what made us [think that it wasn't a bear], because bears aren't typically that tall in the area we were at. We'll get black bears, and maybe the occasional small brown bear that wanders that far down, but black bears are more common. They only stand about four and a half to five feet [tall].

So, we shot at it. Me and this guy named Wolf—that's his legal name—he and I were the two closest and we shot. We were the ones closest to it and either his or my shot landed on it. There was a lot of noise from the guns, so it was hard to tell [what the creature] sounded a lot like. It wasn't the movie gorilla noise, it's like a real gorilla noise but much deeper. Which, again, there was a lot of gun firing and stuff, so that's the best I could describe it from memory.

We didn't see it anymore, so we went to investigate the area, because if it's down then obviously we need to do something about a body—bodies left in the woods aren't good, typically—or, we need to hide the evidence if it's a bear. We didn't see anything, aside from large indentions in the leaves [on the ground] as if something large had been standing there, and blood puddled in the leaves and along some of the trees moving away from the camp. We saw broken branches as high up as about six feet.

That's the story of how I shot bigfoot.

Alana said that, out of their party of "six or seven" people, four of them had firearms, and those who were armed "each shot two to three times."

"All of the guys and myself had a gun," she said. "I had a Colt .45 [and] my friend had a magnum. So, he had the big gun. We're assuming that's what got whatever we shot."

She explained that they were about 30 feet away before opening fire, but it was difficult to see what happened after the shooting started, "because of the commotion and the muzzle flare."

"I didn't see it turn around," Alana said. "I just knew that whatever [was reflecting] the light, the [creature's] eyes, was there and then it wasn't. And then when we went to investigate, we found physical evidence of it running away. There were other limbs further on that were the same height and lower that were broken."

"I didn't see any fur," she added. "I just saw eyes and then blood."

She described the creature's eyes as being a "red-orange" color, and the impressions left in the forest floor as "definitely wider than your standard [8.5" x 11"] book" and "at least twice as long [as a bear's foot]."

"The leaves are really dense through there, so even if we had plaster of Paris or something like that, we wouldn't have been able to make anything, but they looked really big," she said of the tracks. "Everyone agreed it wasn't a bear, but we didn't tell the girls."

Alana said that the experience "terrified" everyone present.

"The girls were really jumpy at any little noise" following the encounter, she said, and the forest remained eerily silent.

"At the time we talked about how quiet it was," she said.

Alana also reported that her friend Wolf had previously encountered bigfoot in the same area, although that sighting was "just that he'd seen something walking through."

Bigfoot sightings are reported with relative frequency on and around Blood Mountain. Three sightings in Union and Lumpkin counties, reported between 1994 and 2009, are currently listed in the Bigfoot Field Researchers Organization's online database, and two additional sightings were submitted to Phantoms & Monsters in 2019 by investigator Dan Maslak.

Personally, I don't agree with shooting living things outside of self-defense or hunting for food, and this case doesn't fall into either category. Cryptozoology is divided on that point when it comes to capturing evidence of cryptids, with those opposed to my view arguing that submitting a body to science for examination would actually help protect the species in the long run, since environmental protections for them could then be put in place. My rebuttal has always been that the current lack of bodies would seem to indicate that cryptids don't really need our protection.

Emily and I are no strangers to bigfoot country ourselves, although our areas of investigation often include an equal amount of high strangeness, and although I'm often armed on our expeditions, it's not because of bigfoot. Humans are the only really dangerous thing you're likely to find in the woods; even bears and mountain lions aren't generally interested in attacking people, and most situations where they might be motivated to do so can be easily avoided. So far, we've yet to encounter a situation wherein the use of a firearm felt necessary, and I hope we never do. That doesn't mean we've never met anything unusual in the forest, though.

CHAPTER 12

HIGH STRANGENESS IN THE KETTLE MORAINE

February of 2019 was the first time we went into the southern unit of the Kettle Moraine State Forest in Wisconsin with our friend Jay Bachochin.

A bright, gibbous moon reflected off the deep snow, illuminating the forest around us and eliminating the need for flashlights.

"I've been coming here for almost two years," Jay said as we prepared to head into the forest. "I've known about Bigfoot since the '70s. I never, ever believed in Bigfoot. It wasn't until 2013 when I went out in the woods, and we kind of heard some real weird, simian-type sounds. And we could not go back to the Wisconsin sound board of all the indigenous animals and identify it. But it sounded simian, and that's when I started going out, and that's when I found the footprints. That's when I had the rocks thrown at me."

Neither the small parking area nor the trail ahead were plowed, but Jay's 4x4 SUV was up to the task of getting us there, and we were dressed for the single-digit February cold, so we trudged intrepidly up the path and deeper into the woods.

The trail that led away from where we parked was buried beneath ankle-deep snow, and we were immediately engulfed in thick rows of pine, cherry, and oak trees to either side. It's here that I first noticed the smell. A musky, rotten odor permeated the air, and I assumed that something must have died nearby. I didn't say anything right away. I wanted someone else to notice it first. It didn't take long.

Our path terminated in a T intersection with a wider, smoother trail that had been tamped down by cross-country skiers, and we turned left to continue deeper into the forest.

"Do you smell that?" Jay asked. "What do you smell?"

"It smells more like an artificial kind of musk...like a heavy garbage smell," Emily replied. "The garbage smell isn't like 'holy crap this is a landfill,' it's more the air around it. It's kind of fishy."

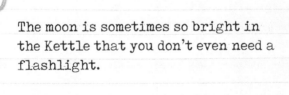

The moon is sometimes so bright in
the Kettle that you don't even need a
flashlight.

IMAGE: Emily Wayland

"It smells like the dump by my parent's house, as you're driving past the landfill," she added.

The smell seemed to fluctuate even as we discussed it, at times overpowering and then suddenly waning to an odorous afterthought.

"Here's the thing," Jay said. "We have sensed this and smelled this out here, and sometimes it's worse than this. I mean, it's enough to make you gag. Then it goes away. Then it comes back. And there's air current here, I get that, but there's really no wind."

He was right. There was no wind to speak of out there. If this was an odor emanating from some stationary mass of refuse, then I don't know how it was so seemingly mobile.

"Take note to see if it follows us," said Jay as we continued along the trail.

We heard dogs barking in the distance then—probably from one of the few houses dotting the landscape—and a short time later the high-pitched howl of a coyote echoed through the forest. An odd, low-pitched howl followed it in response.

"I've never heard that, by the way," Jay said of the low-pitched howl. "You can say the lower one, okay, coyote maybe, but then I've heard so many people and so many accounts of people hearing mimicry. That real low one, that was weird."

Wolves possess a lower howl that might explain it, and they do occasionally range that far south, although it's rare.

We stopped halfway through the large loop we were following through the forest to gather our wits and catch our breath. Emily had been on edge since we arrived. She said she felt unwelcome, a feeling she attributed to whatever was lurking in the woods. The feeling was strongest, she said, whenever the smell that has been following us was its most pungent.

"It freaks me out," she explained. "The smell doesn't scare me, it just happens to be at the same time [as the strong feeling of being un-welcome.]"

As we stood on the trail talking, a sound like the crack of a large stick striking a tree trunk emanated from within the forest. I heard it coming from behind Jay and Emily, who were standing in front of me, but they said it came from behind me. Sound does funny things in the Kettle, and the true origin of the noise was impossible to trace.

"You heard it too, didn't you?" asked Jay.

We nodded. Maybe it was a branch giving way under the strain of ice and snow, but it sure sounded like something struck a tree to me.

I saw something in the trees, then. A light flashed in the treetops some distance away. It reminded me of a camera flash, and I saw a circular white orb in its center before it disappeared. The light was too high up to be a porch light or something similar from a house, and its brief appearance belied that possibility, anyway. Nor could a plane have explained its appearance, unless it was tiny and flying through the trees.

"We've seen them, too. We've seen them here for years," said Jay of the light.

UFOs and orbs are a regular occurrence out there.

"We see UFOs out here, too," Jay said. "You know how you see a satellite in the summer sky? We got them at plane level, and they [fly along] with no sound, just watching. And there's no way it's up near the stars because we saw it go off in the distance, then go off through clouds—so it was in our atmosphere. Whatever it was."

"What else have people seen out here? Lights coming around the corner, that are like flashlights, almost like orbs...on the trail," he continued. "One time, near spring, I was up a kettle path near the bottom, and it turned, you could see the trees, and we're sitting there talking and I'm looking at this orange flashlight coming down the path. I'm like, 'that's weird.' I thought it was a person. I walked down to them right away. We were ready to, you know, meet them. I turned the corner and there was nothing there. It was the weirdest thing."

Jay is a regular visitor to the Kettle Moraine State Forest; all the better to conduct his research. It's his frequent visits that have given him the familiarity necessary to help contextualize what we'd experienced that night.

"I try to get out here weekly," he told us as we followed the trail back to the entrance. "You can do a ghost investigation, but when do you really go back to that location? Six months? A year? But here, I'm out all the time."

The vastness of this area gives him plenty to explore, and Jay's intrepidity gives me hope that his hard work will someday pay off.

"We are in a dot of the Kettle," he said. "You walk down there and turn yourself around a few times, you're lost. This is a speck of the Kettle Moraine. It's immense. And people don't get off the beaten path. People stay on the path, where it's safe."

Since that night, we've gone out with Jay into various parts of that forest over half a dozen times, and we've experienced everything from anomalous balls of light to phantom vocalizations to interesting spirit box messages. On at least one occasion, I spotted what looked like an eight-foot-tall, humanoid shadow cross the trail maybe a hundred or more feet ahead of us. It's a fascinating place full of startling phenomena, but for all that, I've never felt like I was in danger. I bet that if whatever is behind any of the impossible experiences we've examined so far wanted to hurt us, we'd be hurt; simple as that.

CHAPTER 13

THE MADDENING NATURE OF FAERIES

But even for all our collective efforts and experiences, we still don't know what exactly is behind the phenomena happening to so many of us. There are themes that have emerged out of the testimony of witnesses, such as observation and interruption, and times and places when the Other—for lack of a better term to describe these collected intelligences, whatever they are—seems more likely to be encountered. At night, especially when we're near sleep, is a popular time for them to appear, along with when we're travelling or whenever else our conscious minds are distracted. Time and space offer little or no impediment to these beings, nor do physical objects serve as effective barriers; they seem equally likely to visit us in an isolated national forest or the perceived safety of our own home. Regardless of when and where they occur, the experiences often elicit powerful emotions or deliver baffling messages, with no apparent thought given to the welfare of the recipient.

It's strange, but the closest analogue to these collective phenomena that I can come up with is faerie lore, especially since belief in and encounters with faeries began centuries ago yet have persisted into the present day. I don't mean to present faeries as an explanation, that would be no better than handwaving it all away as angels or demons or anything else we can't prove exists. No, I merely want to examine the similarities between the folkloric umbrella encompassing our traditional knowledge of faeries and these seemingly modern high strangeness events which haunt us today. To do so, we must first attempt to understand and define faeries, itself no mean feat, but perhaps in that attempt we might still stumble upon some insight like a wayward traveler blundering into a faerie circle in the dead of night. There are several popular theories to explain the essence of these obfuscated entities, each based on their own belief systems and encumbered by the accompanying dogma thereof, but these explanations are far from definitive.

Wiccans and other pagan sects are known to equate faeries with nature spirits, or elementals, much in the same way that Gnomes—an amalgamation of Nisser, Tomtar, and Dwarfs—were said by Paracelsus to be earth elementals; these communities tend to hold nature in high regard and often claim some connection with various forms of traditional knowledge. It's never been unusual to associate faeries with a particular natural object or location—interesting rock formations, hills, and bodies of water, for instance—but this belief places faeries even further into the natural realm by defining them as expressions of the natural objects themselves.

While there's no denying the association between faeries and the natural world, which is well-established—Pixies are often associated with certain plants, like foxglove, or rings of mushrooms, for instance—one must consider the origin of the narratives that claim these connections. In the agrarian societies so prevalent until little over a century ago, the natural world played a prominent role in people's lives and the average person lived much closer to nature. Nature itself was dangerous and untamed, it was given a significance and authority that few in developed parts of the world feel today. And given the proximity of nature in most people's lives, it would make sense that the natural world be a backdrop for many experiences involving these unusual entities. A chance encounter with a strange creature in the woods could easily take on a special significance, just as they often do today, and a correlation between the creature and its location might be formed.

Similarly, animal husbandry and growing crops were necessary for survival, and these important aspects of our ancestors' lives were closely tied to their interactions with faeries. There could be few more helpful acts than aiding in a harvest or feeding livestock, nor could there be many more harmful than destroying the same. But the behavior of Nisser and Brownies, both of which were said to either help or hinder the performance of chores, based on their mood and temperament, wasn't due to any affinity for farm work so much as their adherence to the particular rules through which they interacted with humanity, and the actions of faeries on homesteads always had more to do with people than plants and animals. When neo-pagans claim that faeries are the literal spirits of natural phenomena, they're simply doing what we've seen many of the witnesses in this book do, the thing that humankind is wont to do when confronting the unexplained: they're applying a narrative to make sense of it. For them, that association with nature provides a context that works within their personal belief system to explain the unexplainable. But that narrative comes from humanity, not the Other, and as we'll see, it has plenty of competition.

Ghosts and hauntings are among the oldest paranormal phenomena to exist in any human culture, and in no aspect of faerie lore is the connection between humans and faeries more pronounced than in the idea that the Fair Folk are spirits of the dead. Nisser and Tomtar were once said to be patriarchal ancestor spirits who remained active to aid in the upkeep of their homestead—especially during certain times of year, like Yule—and were particularly favorable towards those who held their values, like a belief in the virtue of hard work. Dwarfs were also closely associated with the afterlife and were said to sometimes act as guardians of the underworld. Faeries of all stripes are rumored to dwell in and near burial sites and ancient prehistoric forts—haunted barrows and faerie hills are often one and the same, depending on whom you ask. Even a popular retelling of the legend behind the faerie song Paddy's Rambles through the Park has the titular tune first heard in a cemetery, as mentioned earlier.

Correlating faeries and ghosts seems natural enough. The reported behavior of faeries, especially those said to dwell in the home, is strongly similar to ghosts, and poltergeist effects are often reported alongside both. An angry Boggart, for instance, can cause items to fly off the shelf, and will travel with a family if they try to move away—just as some hauntings are said to do. The resemblance between the two phenomena—faeries and hauntings—is disconcerting, and one can hardly be blamed for believing that there may be a root phenomenon at least partially responsible.

But there is another aspect of the unexplained that also deserves examination, one that has enough similarity with both faeries and hauntings to warrant comparison: UFOs and extraterrestrial encounters. Some have speculated that perhaps faeries are beings from another world or dimension, and that our ancestor's interpretation of them was the historical equivalent of modern tales of encounters with alien beings. Almost every subcategory of ufology has an analogue in faerie folklore. Strange lights seen at night were once called will-o'-the-wisps, and the lonely hills and barrows where they were witnessed might today be called window areas. Circles of flattened plants found in fields were once blamed on faeries but have since been rebranded as anonymously created crop circles in the modern era. In his 1911 work The Fairy Faith in Celtic Countries, author W. Y. Evans-Wentz recorded folktales of faeries coming in the night to thresh farmers' grain in a way very similar to 'The Mowing-Devil' of 1678, both phenomena being analogous to modern crop circles. Modern day UFO and abduction experiencers tend to report some of the same haunting phenomena occasionally attributed to faeries, including objects moving on their own and other poltergeist effects.

Faeries had an interest in human reproduction and were reported to steal babies away to replenish their own thinning stock, just as today some extraterrestrials are said to perform hybridization experiments to save their own doomed species. Faeries and extraterrestrials both are often active at night, and love to visit humans as they sleep—the Sidhe were said to abduct people from their beds, just as grey aliens are accused of doing today. But neither is limited to bedroom visitation, and both faeries and extraterrestrials reportedly accost travelers caught unawares.

Consider the following scenario: a person is out walking along a lonely country road when they see strange lights in the distance, they are then approached by short beings who take them away to an otherworldly environment, eventually returning them to roughly the spot they were taken, and the unfortunate victim is later startled to discover that far more time has passed than they thought possible. Is this an encounter with faeries or extraterrestrials? Reported interactions with both often contain one or more of these listed elements, and while some superficial details—the beings' appearance, method of travel, etc.—might differ, the predominant narrative is the same.

Few experiences encapsulate the relationship between faeries and UFO lore better than the one had by Joe Simonton, who encountered three otherworldly beings in the spring of 1961; an event that would play out almost identically to tales of faeries told throughout history. Had Simonton known what the result of this event would be that late morning on his chicken farm in Eagle River, Wisconsin, he likely would have simply locked his door, drawn the shades, and been done with the whole ordeal.

The following is Simonton's story, according to an excerpt from Jacques Vallée's *Passport to Magonia*. Vallée was an early proponent of connecting faerie lore and UFO reports, and *Passport to Magonia* is essential reading for anyone interested in the subject.

The time was approximately 11:00 A.M. on April 18, 1961, when Joe Simonton was attracted outside by a peculiar noise similar to "knobby tires on a wet pavement." Stepping into his yard, he faced a silvery saucer-shaped object "brighter than chrome," which appeared to be hovering close to the ground without actually touching it. The object was about twelve feet high and thirty feet in diameter. A hatch opened about five feet from the ground, and Simonton saw three men inside the machine. One of them was dressed in a black two-piece suit. The occupants were about five feet in height. Smooth shaven, they appeared to "resemble Italians." They had dark hair and skin and wore outfits with turtleneck tops and knit helmets.

One of the men held up a jug apparently made of the same material as the saucer. His motions to Joe Simonton seemed to indicate that he needed water. Simonton took the jug, went inside the house, and filled it. As he returned, he saw that one of the men inside the saucer was "frying food on a flameless grill of some sort." The interior of the ship was black, "the color of wrought iron." Simonton, who could see several instrument panels, heard a slow whining sound, similar to the hum of a generator. When he made a motion indicating he was interested in the food that was being prepared, one of the men, who was also dressed in black but with a narrow red trim along the trousers, handed him three cookies, about three inches in diameter and perforated with small holes.

The whole affair had lasted about five minutes. Finally, the man closest to the witness attached a kind of belt to a hook in his clothing and closed the hatch in such a way that Simonton could scarcely detect its outline. Then the object rose about twenty feet from the ground before taking off straight south, causing a blast of air that bowed some nearby pine trees.

This odd encounter has been catalogued alongside many other high strangeness cases in the annals of ufology, although, upon careful reflection, incidents such as Simonton's have much more in common with the faerie stories of our ancestors than what one would expect from interstellar visitors.

Many faerie stories include strange sounds or music being heard before encountering the fey near one of their hill fortresses or out in procession, and Simonton's "knobby tires on a wet pavement" might have been described as the staccato beat of a drumline in a different era. Often faeries are said to be encountered near lonely hills or prehistoric ruins, but traversing the wilderness is not the only way to encounter the good folk; many tales exist of faerie encounters that take place in farmsteads and cottages—farms not too different from Simonton's. But Simonton's encounter doesn't seem to have much in common with house-dwelling faeries, such as Brownies and Hobgoblins, so much as a chance encounter with the Fair Folk.

There is a tale, popular in faerie lore, of a helpful ploughman who, upon finding a broken faerie spade on Wick Moor, mended the fey implement and was rewarded by his grateful Good Neighbors with a gift of faerie-made cakes. Faeries rewarding a helpful human with food is not uncommon in folklore, and Simonton's experience mirrors that of the stories. Simonton's offering of water to his unexpected guests is certainly well-received, and he is similarly rewarded with a gift of food, in this case, the traditional faerie cakes.

Unlike their folkloric counterparts, however, Simonton's cakes were delivered to a lab where they could be studied. The faerie food was brought to the Food and Drug Laboratory of the U.S. Department of Health, Education, and Welfare as part of an investigation by the Air Force's Project Bluebook.

According to the lab's examination,

The cake was composed of hydrogenated fat, starch, buckwheat hulls, soya bean hulls, wheat bran. Bacteria and radiation readings were normal for this material. Chemical, infra-red and other destructive type tests were run on the material. The Food and Drug Laboratory of the U.S. Department of Health, Education and Welfare concluded that the material was an ordinary pancake of terrestrial origin.

So, it was concluded that there wasn't anything necessarily out of the ordinary about Simonton's cakes, other than the method with which they were supposedly delivered. It is not necessarily unusual for one to receive a gift of relatively unremarkable food in return for aiding faeries. In traditional folklore, these gifts are much better received than the cursed and glamoured food one might be offered in a faerie hill or celebration. Unlike the latter, a well-earned gift from the Fair Folk doesn't come with any negative metaphysical repercussions, and this held true with Simonton, whose curse came not from any faerie spell, but from the banality of his peer's beliefs.

In accepting this gift, Joe Simonton had been cursed; not by the magic of the fey, but with the ridicule brought by exposing such a story to the materialist paradigm. By all accounts, Simonton was a well-regarded and upstanding member of his community prior to the event, and certainly not a man taken to flights of fancy. However, weeks after his encounter, in an interview with a United Press International reporter, he declared that "if it happened again, I don't think I'd tell anybody about it."

The Air Force had decided that Simonton had fallen victim to a "waking dream," and despite his insistence on the veracity of his claims, he was not taken seriously by many who heard his tale. The effect that this dismissiveness has on witnesses of the impossible is often emotionally devastating, and quite understandably discourages many people from ever coming forward.

We should be thankful for the Joe Simontons of the world. Without people like him, and their strange stories of the impossible, our knowledge of the bizarre circumstances of our shared world would be much less complete. Transactions between humanity and such strange species as previously described did not start with the UFO age and forcing experiences such as Simonton's into as inadequate a category as that of UFO contactee is harmful in its reductionism. That these stories continue a tradition of interaction with some unknowable intelligence is no coincidence, and the truth of it may be the key to truly understanding the Other. But left unexamined, we will never know.

The 14th century Middle English wodewose, or wild man, deserves to be mentioned here as well. These hairy humanoids were often compared to forest spirits or faeries in the Germanic cultures and would seem analogous to the Bigfoot of today. Bigfoot themselves are no strangers to high strangeness according to modern eyewitness accounts, as documented in Joshua Cutchin and Timothy Renner's excellent two-volume series on the subject, Where the Footprints End, not to mention personally experienced by Emily and me while investigating areas said to house the mysterious beings. Strange lights, disembodied voices, and even missing time all exist on the periphery of the Bigfoot phenomenon, just as they do everything from ghosts to faeries to UFOs.

There are plenty of other proposed explanations for faeries, too, from partially fallen angels to ancestral memories of flesh-and-blood little people who once inhabited the prehistoric structures where they are often said to be seen. But those tend to ignore the associations described herein, and while they might offer partial explanations, they tend not to speak to the heart of the mystery. What people once called faeries appears to be something so broad and deep that it encompasses aspects of almost all paranormal phenomena by which we are still haunted today, and in fact, given the varied and often monstrous descriptions of faeries throughout history, practically any of the beings we've seen encountered in this work could be linked to them in one form or another.

As I wrote in *The Lake Michigan Mothman: High Strangeness in the Midwest:*

> There's some aspect of this phenomenon that is enormous and just out of sight, a depth of paranormality concealed beneath the surface of consensus reality. And it touches everything, connecting it—UFOs, ghosts, cryptids, magick, all of it. A common explanation for faeries used to be that they were the souls of the dead. What if we actually can become faeries when we die? What if we can become mothmen?
>
> What if that connective force just beneath the surface is consciousness itself: a universal consciousness that our brains merely act as antennae to receive, and upon which our personalities and unique consciousnesses are imprinted like waves in an ocean; individual, yet still part of the whole. Sensory organs for the universe to experience itself. Keel called this force the "superspectrum." What if, once we fully realize the inherent abilities thereof, we become privy to vast new expanses of existence and probability? Whole new vistas of post-human experience would reveal themselves.
>
> Perhaps what we're dealing with is a species more native than we to this hidden reality, a being or beings with an unimaginably expansive reach, wielding power too vast for us to understand, and capable of effortless manipulation. Like a shark they effortlessly traverse this ocean in all dimensions, utterly alien to our understanding,

while we are doomed to flounder. Maybe there's something that we call faeries or ghosts or extraterrestrials but is something else entirely; something with which humanity has been interacting for a very long time that has, at different times, gone by many different names, or has at least been interpreted by us in many different ways. In this ecology of consciousness there might be a variety of inhabitants, of whom any may or may not have been misidentified to some extent throughout the ages. I still allow for the individualization of paranormal phenomena; I'm open to the idea of human consciousness surviving bodily death, after all. However, human consciousnesses—whether currently inhabiting a body or not—could represent a relatively minor portion of the population.

The truth of this being or beings is completely unknown or, far more unsettlingly, perhaps it is unknowable. Not because it's impossible for the human mind to comprehend it, but rather, because they don't want us to know.

And so, we are left with a phenomenon that we seem to be no closer to understanding than we were at its advent in our far distant past; a phenomenon that must, for now, remain a mystery, since we may lack the means to properly perceive it.

CHAPTER 14

BLACK SHEEP

And yet, hope is not lost. We still have each other and our shared experiences, and I have always been a believer in the triumph of the human spirit. So much of these phenomena seem to occur using consciousness, at least in part, as a medium and we're only now even considering the untapped potential contained within human consciousness. There may yet be ways for us to use this to our advantage, or at least level the playing field, when interacting with these entities. Perhaps our ancestors' magickal and spiritual practices aren't the products of outdated philosophies that materialism would have us believe. And until we've regained and hopefully improved upon such abilities, we still have each other to lean on. When I consider the comfort that we can provide each other in this regard, I'm reminded of a conversation I had with my Uncle Joe before he passed.

For the longest time I considered myself the black sheep of my family. I thought that I was alone in my experiences, the only one to witness the impossible. But the older I get the more cracks appear in the normality of our middle-class facade, and strange, dark, unknowable things slip through to confront the comforting light of consensus reality. The truth is there's no such thing as normal, and the labels we apply to ourselves are often just lies we tell to convince us that the madness we experience is at least a local phenomenon, that there's still someplace safe where we can hide, some refuge from the existential terror of things we can't understand—but no such place exists, we're just people, and the paranormal universe envelops us all.

I hadn't spoken to my Uncle Joe outside of social media, text messages, and the occasional quick phone conversation over the holidays, since my grandmother's funeral a few years before; not for any particular reason, it was just that he lived in Texas, and I was in Wisconsin, and life just kept speeding up. Time is a commodity that I now regret squandering in my youth. So, I was glad when he contacted me about a couple of UFO experiences he had when he was a young man, since I could say I was being productive and catch up with one of my favorite relatives at the same time.

My Uncle Joe grew up in rural Illinois with three sisters, including my mother. They didn't have much money, and the difficulties endemic to country poverty made them stoic and practical—they don't put on airs, and they aren't prone to flights of fancy.

We spent some time catching up, as people do, but before long we were talking about ghost lights.

"It was probably 1959 or 1960—whenever my grandpa Hartley died, it was right after that," Joe said. "We were living on the Smith place—which is gone now—out east of Bardolph [Illinois] in an old farmhouse, and we had one of them couches that makes out to a bed, downstairs."

I was sleeping on it and mom, dad, and the girls were all upstairs. Well, I was lying there trying to go to sleep, and of course out in the country it's real dark, and all of a sudden, I seen this thing come through the wall and I thought "What in the heck is that?"

It was round, and it looked...it was perfectly round, it didn't have a corona or anything like that going from it—it was just perfectly round. The inside of it looked like fire, not like a candle, but...it was edge to edge, that's what it was, that's what it reminded me of, the orangish little temperature fire. And it stayed there, and it hovered around, it looped around a little bit, and I don't know, probably 10 minutes later it just...poof, took off.

Like many of us who have experienced the impossible, my uncle was at a loss to explain the experience.

"And I have no idea, I haven't seen anything like that since," he said.

But that's not the strangest story he shared with me that evening. Uncle Joe also related to me a UFO sighting he had back in the late 1960s when he was around 12 years old.

"This is where it gets creepy," he began. "When we lived out on the Fiddler farm, which is just east of the Bardolph blacktop, there used to be a farm there on the northside of 136 right past the Bardolph blacktop. It was probably afternoon. It was warm weather, because I remember having a t-shirt and shorts on. But it had to be late summer or early fall because the sun was about in the center, you know what I mean? Like the equinox had already been here."

I remember looking at the sky, which was perfectly blue. There may have been a stray cloud a ways away or something like that, but as far as visibility it was blue. I seen this black dot, and it came from the northeast in an arc, and it came over and stopped. I thought okay that must be a helicopter.

Well, it stayed there, didn't move; didn't get bigger, didn't get smaller, stayed there. No contrail, no fire, smoke, nothing like that. And I would estimate it if I triangulated it from me off of the ground it was about 30-40 degrees. It was close enough that I could see the texture of whatever it was.

I watched that thing for probably, oh god, twenty minutes, a half hour—something like that. And it stayed in that one spot that long. And then all of a sudden it took off to the northwest in basically the same type of ark, and it was gone.

On the surface it seemed simple enough—a fairly standard UFO sighting with a typically unsatisfying resolution, but as always, the devil here was lodged firmly in the details.

"Now, as far as any missing time or anything like that I wouldn't have any idea. I don't think I was abducted or anything like that. I'm not a crazy person," he said. "The texture of it is what got me, it wasn't a regular silver flying saucer like everybody sees or nothing like that. It had the texture of a rock or a—and this is going to sound stupid—but you know how a meatball looks? It's got that rough looking texture? That's what the surface of this looked like."

It gets weirder.

"And the thing of it was, I wasn't scared," Joe explained. "Matter of fact, I had a—this is going to sound crazy, too—I had an overwhelming feeling of belonging, and don't ask me why. I don't know."

"The thing that really fascinated me is that it just stopped, like it was just looking at something," he added. "There wasn't any sound, which was another really weird thing."

And we were once again left with no explanation. I could at least commiserate, given my own experiences.

"I've been scratching my head about it for over half a century and I have no idea what it was," said Joe.

I get it.

So many witnesses to the impossible understand what it is to be left with nothing but the maddening frustration of curiosity bereft of explanation. It's a common feeling shared by those who witness unexplained phenomena, and if nothing else, it was nice to hear another of my blood relatives understood it. At least we understand something.

ABOUT THE AUTHOR

Tobias Wayland is a passionate fortean who has been actively investigating the unusual for over a decade; the first several years of his investigative career were spent as a MUFON field investigator, and following that he investigated independently prior to becoming the head writer and editor for the Singular Fortean Society. Tobias is a frequent guest on various podcasts and radio shows, has contributed to several books on the paranormal, and is often invited to speak at paranormal conferences and events. He was also featured in the Small Town Monsters documentary *Terror in the Skies* and the series premiere of Expedition X for his work investigating Mothman sightings around Lake Michigan. He and his wife Emily have been involved with the Lake Michigan Mothman investigation since its advent in the spring of 2017, and recently published a book chronicling the experience, *The Lake Michigan Mothman: High Strangeness in the Midwest.*

His years as an investigator have served him best by illustrating that when it comes to the anomalous, the preternatural, and the paranormal, any answers he's found are still hopelessly outnumbered by questions.

singularfortean.com

Follow us on social media: *@singularfortean*

Printed in Great Britain
by Amazon